Tales o

Other counties in this series include:

Tales of Old Sussex

~

Lillian Candlin

With illustrations by Don Osmond

COUNTRYSIDE BOOKS
NEWBURY, BERKSHIRE

First Published 1985
© Lillian Candlin 1985
Reprinted 1986, 1987
Reprinted 1990, 1992 and 1999

COUNTRYSIDE BOOKS
3 CATHERINE ROAD
NEWBURY, BERKSHIRE

ISBN 0905392 45 0

Designed by Mon Mohan

Produced through MRM Associates Ltd., Reading
Printed in England by J. W. Arrowsmith Ltd., Bristol

To Judyth, Jane, Patricia,
Peter and Barry

Contents

SUSSEX – The map overleaf is by John Speede and shows
the county as it was in the early seventeenth century

CHICHESTER

SUSSE
Described
divided int
pes with th
ation of Ch
ter the che
citie thereof

PART

Defcribed by IO1
Speede And are
the Exchange by

A S. Martynes	I S. Peters	R East Gate
B The Tollhoue	K. Paradice	S S. Pancras
C Tollouse ftreet	L Eaft lane	T S. Bartholmer
D Blackfryers	M Counlane	V Aquiltry Bridge
E S. Andrews	N VVeght lane	W South Gate
F S. Maryes Hofpi	X S. Teckes	X North Gate
G Grayfryers	Y S. Ricketh vpo	
H The Pallace	Q Our Ladye chap	

Part of   OF

SUR   REY

Hantfhire

WEST

Lowell Crofte

worth
worth

Forest

nant Forest

BRAM

BER RAPE

LEWE

TER
CICHES

ARONDELL   RAPE

Petworth

RAPE

Arondell Foreft

Arundell

Terring

CHICHESTER

RAPE

THE

The marfhoue

Selfey Peninfu

Bognor Rocks

WILLIAM de
Albania Earle
of Chichefter
and Arundell.

IOHN FITZ
Allan Earle of Suf
fex et Arundell.

The Scale of miles

| 1 | 2 | 3 | 4 | 5 | 6 | 7 | 8 |

Jodocus Hon

PART OF KENT.

DIEV ET MON DROIT

PEVENSEY RAPE

HASTINGS RAPE

Oxney Island

Pevensey Mershe

BRITISH SEA

WILLIAM the Baſtard, Duke of Normandy, making his Clayme to the Crowne of England, by affinitye, adoption and promiſe, arined as a port in Suſſex called Penſey with 896 ſhips furniſhed for warre the 28 of September, ý yere of Chriſts incarnation 1066. And the 14 of October following being Satterdays, nere Neighton in ý ſame Coūtie ý had battayll with Harald King of England, whoe in ý feilde valliantly fighting was there ſlaine by the ſhote of an arrow into his brayne: and with him lyed Gerth and Leofwine his brethren, and 67974 men bißdes. The place where they fought, ever ſince doth in memory thereof beare the name of Battayll, where the Heptarchie of the ſaxōs was Brought to ý laſt period. Hauing all their limes altered, their Nobles diſplaced, and all men diſhonored and ſeaſed into the Normāds hands, whoe made him ſelf Lorde of all, and on ý dayes of Chriſtmas natiuitye in ſ ſame yere was crowned at weſtminſter King of England, which he gouerned the ſpace of 20 yeres, 8 mounthus, and 16. dayes.

PHILLIP Howard Earle of Arundell.

ROBERT Radcliffe Earle of Suſſex

Domini 1610.

Dragons
in the
Sussex Forests

S ussex has always had the reputation of being a land
where huge dragons and serpents lived.

The *Anglo-Saxon Chronicle*, written in the 8th century, speaks
of 'wondrous adders that were to be seen in the land of the
South Saxons'. Ethelward's *Chronicle* of 770 AD records that
'monstrous serpents were seen in the country of the Southern
Angles that is called Sussex'.

To this day when the Sussex Tipteerers (mummers) go
around at Christmastide, they are accompanied by a dragon
who runs around snapping his great jaws and frightening
small children out of their wits. I remember one Boxing Day,
when I went with a small boy of three years of age looking for
the Tipteerers. Just as we got out of the car, the dragon rushed
towards us and snapped his fearful mouth. The boy gave a
scream and no one could pacify him, so back into the car we
had to get and drive away. The night was followed by more
screaming fits as the boy remembered afresh the horrible
creature!

The forest of Andrieda, in early times, lay at the foot of the
Downs on the north side, and stretched from east to west for
almost the whole length of Sussex, and went as far as the
northern border.

Parts of the forest, right up to the 16th century, had never
been surveyed. Even in these days of land shortage there still
remain beautiful lonely spots which are known to few people,
though the forest has now dwindled somewhat. Towns,
villages and roads have eaten into it. But seven separate pieces

remain: Ashdown, St Leonards, Faygate, Balcombe, Tilgate, Worth and Sheffield, and many large pieces of woodland still remain. In three of these forests stories of dragons roaming around are told.

On the water meadows at Lyminster, within sight of Arundel Castle, a great water monster lived in what is known as the 'knucker' or 'nicor' hole. The tale attached to the knucker hole is centuries old, it certainly goes back to Saxon times, because the word 'nicor' is the Saxon word for a water monster.

The actual site of the knucker hole is almost at the foot of the little hill on which Lyminster Church now stands. It is a large pool continuously freshened by underground springs and is level with the surrounding water meadows. From this pool the dragon was said to come periodically for food. The only food that it liked, however, was a fair damsel, and fair damsels were in short supply in Sussex; in fact, the only one left was the daughter of the King of Sussex. The king, naturally not wanting his daughter to be eaten, gave out a proclamation that he would give his daughter in marriage plus half of his kingdom to anyone who would come and kill the beast.

A brave knight, just returned from service overseas, answered the call and came along to have a try. He waited around the hole and when next the dragon came up for food he set about him and in an heroic fight he killed him stone dead, but not before the knight had been injured. As in all good stories, he was of course nursed by the beautiful daughter of the king.

That is one version of how the knucker died. But some folk say the beast was killed by trickery. In some stories it was by means of a huge Sussex pie, so big in fact that it had to be drawn to the side of the hole in a large farm cart. Its savoury smell brought the creature out of the hole. He gave one sniff and promptly swallowed pie, plus the cart and horse! Alas, however, the pie was full of poison and the knucker curled up and died in agony.

Yet another version of this story which appeared in the *Sussex County Magazine* in 1926, written by Charles Joiner, said that it was a Sussex suet pudding that tempted the knucker out of his hole. This also had to be drawn by horse and cart to the pool and was made by one Jim Pulk, the man who in several tales is said to have been the slayer. In this version Jim puts something in the pudding that gives old knucker the collywobbles and while he is rolling about in pain up comes Jim with a large pill to cure him quickly. Knucker takes the pill and while he is about to swallow it, Jim ups with an axe and chops off his head.

In the south transept of Lyminster church is an ancient gravestone which is known as 'The Slayer's Stone' (the stone of the man who slew the creature). The stone was previously in the churchyard, and fifty years ago local children used to say that the little ridges on it (which had in fact been formed by centuries of rain running over it) were made by the dragon trying to get at the body of his slayer.

The Knucker Hole, I am pretty sure, was once a magic (religious) pool of our pagan ancestors. These people worshipped everything that gave life. Water, of course, was one of these things and so had to be placated with gifts. Special pools, rivers and streams were set aside where sacrifices could be made.

The water of the knucker hole was reputed to have magic qualities within living memory. People have told me that they remember a man coming to the pool and filling little bottles with the water, and that he took it away and sold it as a cure for all ills.

The pool would have been magic to the early people because the water hardly changes temperature. In the great freeze-up of 1961-2, little birds were bathing in the water while all around the land and water was frozen solid.

It was also claimed that the hole was bottomless. Some years ago, members of the Brighton & Hove Sub-Aqua Club explored it under the direction of Con. Ainsworth, a well-known Sussex archaeologist. A depth of thirty feet was reached before mud was found, from which gushed powerful streams of fresh water, that for many years had fed watercress beds.

The first nunnery to be opened in Sussex is probably

responsible for the knucker legend. The nuns would have taught that the pond was out-of-bounds to converts and that God did not need their pagan sacrifices. Dragons, especially green ones, were used for many years by the Church as a symbol of evil. In the minds of the people this fact would have been linked with the pool, and before long the evil dragon and the pool would have become connected.

There are no accounts in this country of 'fair maidens' being sacrificed though animals certainly were. But it is conceivable that at a time of great drought, such as when St Wilfred came to Sussex, a girl was offered as sacrifice and the folk memory survived.

Alas! Whatever the truth of this, no longer can children be taken to the knucker hole to be thrilled by the story of the dragon who once lurked there. The pool has now been enclosed with high wooden fencing, and it is now part of a fishery for breeding trout.

St Leonard's Forest, near Horsham, had a dragon shaped like a huge lizard, to whom, it is said, we owe the beauty and fragrance of the lily-of-the-valley. These flowers still grow wild in the forest, but now they are protected by the Wild Flower Society. The spot where they grow is known as 'the Lily beds', and Sussex maps issued before the First World War have the spot marked as such.

The legend here is that a fearsome creature used to wander around looking for its prey. One day the people of Horsham noticed that it was getting nearer and nearer to their town, and they prayed aloud that someone would come and rid them of the creature.

Good St Leonard heard their prayers. He came down to Sussex, and after searching the forest he eventually came upon the fearsome dragon. A terrible fight ensued in which the saint finally overcame the beast, but in the process the saint lost a lot of blood. Wherever a drop of his blood fell, lily-of-the-valley sprang up.

The lily-of-the-valley has long been thought to have the power to bring good, and it has figured in legends ever since men have been telling tales. Dedicated to the Norse Goddess Ostarta, the flower was dedicated to Our Lady when

Christianity arrived here, and given the folk name of 'Our Lady's Tears'.

Of the third dragon, which is said to have roamed between St Leonard's Forest and Faygate Forest, in the 17th century, we have an authentic account. This tale reads something like the hunt for the Loch Ness Monster!

Around 1600 rumours about a dragon being seen here began to circulate beyond the confines of Sussex, and one can imagine how, whenever there was a report about it having been seen, much speculation must have arisen as to whether it really existed or not.

The tale eventually came to the ears of one John Trundle, a London man, who decided to investigate the truth or otherwise of the story. He made a journey into Sussex, and in those days it really was something of a journey because of the mud that made any travelling in the Weald impossible at times. He interviewed the four people who claimed they had seen the monster. These were an unnamed carrier who plied between Horsham and the White Horse Inn at Southwark, a John Steel, a Christopher Horder, and a widow woman who lived near Faygate.

That all four agreed on the shape, size and habits of the creature, when people were illiterate, speaks for itself. It is hardly likely that all four could have invented such similar descriptions.

John Trundle, in 1614, published his findings in a pamphlet entitled *A True and Wonderful Discourse relating to a strange and monstrous Serpent (or Dragon) lately discovered, and yet living, to the great Annoyance* . . .

One of these pamphlets is now in the Harleian Miscellany, and in it the creature is described as being nine feet long, with a body shaped like the 'axel-tree of a cart' – thick in the middle and smaller at both ends (i.e., lizard shaped) – covered with black scales and with a powerful tail. It is said that at the sound of man or cattle it will raise its long neck, supposed to be an ell long (45 inches) and look around with great arrogance. It does not, however, appear to eat either man or cattle.

Because of the similarity of the descriptions given, the four independent witnesses must have seen *something*. This something could possibly have been a descendant of a prehistoric monster that had managed to live on long after such animals were thought to have become extinct, surviving in the unexplored depths of the forest.

Curiously enough, their descriptions fit uncannily well with that of the largest lizard in the world found by David Attenborough when he went in search of a dragon in the 1960s. He found it on Komodo, a very remote island in the Indonesian Archipelago. The Komodo dragon, described by David Attenborough in his book *Zoo Quest for a Dragon*, is twelve feet long, shaped like a lizard, covered with black scales, has four short legs and a powerful tail that can knock a man down. It lifts its head on a long neck when its curiosity is aroused and 'the line of his savage mouth curved upwards in a fixed sardonic grin and from its half-closed jaws an enormous yellow-pink forked tongue, unceasingly slid in and out'. The colour of its tongue and its coming in and out could have given rise to the tale that our Sussex dragon breathed fire.

The Komodo dragon is said to be a descendant of a prehistoric lizard, whose fossil remains have been found in Australia. The fossil remains of a prehistoric animal known as the iguanodon have been found near Faygate. These were found in Tilegate Forest in 1825 by Gidean Mantell. Fossil remains of the iguanodon were also found between January 1939 and February 1941 in the Clock House Brick Works, about six miles from Horsham.

Who is to say, therefore, that a giant lizard, or lizards, could not have lived in the great Wealden forest long after they were thought to be extinct? If this is the case, John Trundle did a great service to posterity when he published his report in 1614. But for him the facts behind the Faygate Dragon legend might well have been lost to Sussex folklore.

Mad Jack Fuller

S quire John Fuller, of Rose Hill, Brightling, near Heathfield, was born in 1757, into a wealthy family of iron founders. A large part of their wealth had come from the making of large guns. A close relation, another John Fuller, wrote in 1749, 'There is Brede, Beckly, Lamberhurst, Robertsbridge, Ashburnham and my own; they are the only furnaces that can make great guns'.

Squire Fuller, however, had no need to work, and the principal thing for which he is still remembered in Sussex is the building of follies on his estate at Brightling Park. It was for this that he acquired the name of 'Mad' Jack Fuller. The best known of these follies is the one that stands black and serene, on the top of a hill that is 640 feet above sea level. This obelisk is known as Brightling Needle, and is a famous landmark. Mad Jack will certainly not be forgotten for as long as the Needle still stands.

Why Jack built the Needle on this spot is not known, but it was probably built to replace a beacon that had previously stood here. Brightling beacon, one of a series all along the Sussex coast, was guarded night and day, and kept ready for firing in the late 18th century, during the expected invasion by Napoleon. It may be that Fuller put it up in thankfulness that Napoleon failed to invade.

This part of Britain has always been the most vulnerable when invasions have been expected. It certainly was during the expected coming of Hitler in the Second World War.

Another of Fuller's follies stands in a field at Woods Corner, in the adjoining parish of Dallington. This is a conical obelisk, surmounted by a ball cap, and although it was built to resemble the spire of Dallington church, it quickly acquired

17

the name of Sugar Loaf, because of its likeness to the shape in which sugar was delivered to grocers in those days. The loaves were large pointed blocks of sugar that had to be chipped into small pieces by hand.

This folly was built as a result of a wager. Fuller boasted about how many spires he could see from his house. When challenged as to whether he could see Dallington spire, he said he could and made a wager that this was so. But when he returned home and found that it was not, he quickly got some workmen together and bribed them to build a mock spire in a single day. Whether he won the wager is not known.

Inside the sugar loaf is a small room. In the 1930s an old man used to tell how he once lived in it and brought up a family there!

In the grounds of Rose Hill is a delightful little circular domed Grecian Temple. It is a single room encircled by a Doric colonnade on a base, approached by a flight of steps. Sir Robert Smirke designed it and according to local gossip, it was used for gambling parties whenever Fuller had guests. Smirke also designed an observatory for Fuller, in which were astronomical and other instruments. This building today has been made into a private house.

But by far the most famous and most written about folly is the large Pyramidical Mausoleum, also designed by Smirke to the wishes of Fuller, which dominates Brightling churchyard. This is big enough to support a legend (which, in all likelihood, was started by Mad Jack himself, long before his death).

The tale goes that inside the monument, Mad Jack sits with a bottle of claret, surrounded by a wide circle of broken glass to protect him from the clutches of the Devil. According to Jack, broken glass was abhorrent to the Devil because it cut his tender hooves.

Some years ago, this tale was refuted by the then vicar, who issued a statement that Fuller had been buried in the same conventional way as other men.

Fuller's follies, however, were not such mad projects as is sometimes thought. They were built at a time when there was a great deal of unemployment. Fuller's way of dealing with this was to give the job of building follies to the local unemployed men. To casual labourers travelling the road in search of work he would give a meal and money for building so many feet of a wall, built of rose coloured bricks, which he hoped in time would encircle the whole of his estate. The colour pink was to commemorate the fact that an ancestress, Elizabeth Fulke-Rose, left to the family large estates in Jamaica.

Another thing for which Mad Jack is remembered in the village is that the Fullers' Arms Inn is not in Brightling at all. At one time it stood at the entrance to Rose Hill, but for some reason or other the landlord offended Fuller and so he got the inn removed to its present site outside the parish. An incident which shows how powerful squires could be in those times.

Fuller was fond of music and he presented the church with a barrel organ which still stands in the church. He took a great interest in the music in the church and in the choir, but when the choir once did something that he did not agree with, he went off and bought nine bassoons, which he presented to the church.

In 1801, Fuller entered Parliament. He sat for his own constituency from 1801 to 1812, and during that time he was offered a peerage by Pitt. This peerage was for his philanthropy. Fuller gave, among other things, £10,000 to the Royal Institute of Great Britain, founded two professorships, and gave a peal of eight bells to the church.

Fuller, however, refused the peerage, saying 'I was born Jack Fuller and Jack Fuller I'll die'. For this reason he is sometimes remembered as 'Honest' Jack Fuller.

From the history of Fuller's days in Parliament, the peerage was probably offered to him because the members of the House of Commons wanted him removed to the House of Lords. He was certainly troublesome at times. Once he had to be carried shouting and struggling out of the House by the Serjeant-at-Arms and his minions, for refusing to give way during a debate, and calling the Speaker 'that insignificant little fellow in a wig'.

Again during a debate on the abolition of slavery, Fuller became very heated and refused to sit down when ordered to do so by the Speaker. Finally he swore at the Speaker and walked out of the House. The Abolition of Slavery Bill, it must be remembered, would have affected his interests in the Jamaica estates which he owned.

In spite of all his mad deeds, however, he did two great things which we should be thankful for. He bought Bodiam Castle, when it was about to be demolished, and saved it for future generations to enjoy, and he was a patron of Turner, one of the greatest of English painters.

Fuller was an eccentric of eccentrics. A man of immense girth, it is said that he once turned the scales at 22 stones! His style of dress was old-fashioned and astounding. He powdered his hair and wore it in a long queque tied with a ribbon bow at a time when this was quite outmoded. It is said of him that he once expressed surprise when a man who did not know him picked him out from a crowd of people. When travelling he always set out in his own coach complete with footman and coachman fully armed with pistol and sword.

Fuller died at the age of 77, in 1834. Whether he deserved the title 'Mad', or 'Honest' is open to doubt, but he must have brought colour and excitement to village life when times were hard and dull for people who worked on the land. His follies still bring interest to people's lives today. Many people go to have a look at his pyramidical tomb in Brightling churchyard, and stand around debating whether the story is true that Jack sits upright within.

Descendants of Jack Fuller lived on in Rose Villa until 1879, when it was sold to Percy Trew who changed the name back to Brightling Park. When his son Thomas Percy died in 1953, the property was sold, and in 1955 the house, like so many Country Houses, was found to be too large for modern times and about half of it was demolished.

The Gooders Go-Gooding

C hristmas has always been a traditional time for giving,
and even today a special effort is made by everyone to
see that those in need have a few little extras to cheer them up
over what is a festive but usually cold season. One of the nicest
customs in the past years took place in late December, just
before Christmas.

St. Thomas' Day, December 21st, was Gooding Day, and
on this day the 'Gooders' turned out in full force to collect
goods for the Christmas feast.

M. A. Lower, the Sussex historian, writing in 1861,
describes how 'Formerly the old women of every parish went
from house to house to beg something to provide for the
festivities of Christmas. The miller gave each dame a little
flour, the grocer a few raisins, the butcher an odd bit of beef,
and so on. From persons not in trade a donation in money was
expected.' He goes on to say that the custom was practically
obsolete as early as 1851.

It must have been quite a sight in the old days to see all the
elderly ladies (it seems to have been only done by the women)
going from house to house around the villages and towns
collecting up the goodies.

Sometimes the event appears to have been something of a
social occasion. John Erridge, in his *History of Brighthelmstone*
(1861), writes that he well remembered as a boy seeing old
Phoebe Hessell, (a woman who had become famous for
fighting in the battle of Fontleroy under the Duke of
Cumberland) sitting in his mother's kitchen, eating a large

slice of cake and washing it down with a glass of his mother's home-made elderberry wine on Gooding Days.

E. Bell-Irving, in her book on Mayfield, published in 1903, says that a few old ladies continue to make their round on Gooding Day, and reports that one old parishioner used to save all his fourpenny pieces to give to the 'Gooders' when they visited him.

My mother, who was born in 1870, when speaking about the old days, would tell how when she was a child there was a big box of shop-soiled clothes outside a drapers in the Cliff High Street at Lewes, labelled 'For the Gooders'.

She liked to tell how one Gooding Day when she was coming home from school with a bigger girl, she was persuaded to take home a hat (or rather a bonnet, as it was in those days) for her mother. Her mother was not pleased. In fact, she was very annoyed to think that a child of hers should be seen carrying home something that was meant for the 'Gooders'.

In the country districts the Gooders visited the 'Big Houses' and here large amounts of goods were doled out. Henry Burstow, a Horsham shoemaker, a kindly man who was interested in all the doing of his fellow townsmen, published in 1911 his memories of his early days in Horsham. In this he gives an account of some of the houses that were visited and what was given.

For example, Sir Timothy Shelley, the father of Shelley the poet, who lived at Field Place gave away large quantities of beef. R. Aldridge, of St. Leonards, gave 6lb. of beef and a plum pudding to about 60 or 70 families. Mr. Fox, of Chestnut Lodge, gave a $\frac{1}{4}$lb. of tea and half-a-crown (12$\frac{1}{2}$p) to 80 old ladies, 2oz. of tea and a shilling (5p) to some 200 more. Many other people gave clothing such as caps, stockings, etc.

At one time when the Gooders had done the rounds of the houses and shops they moved on to the church, where money willed by former parishioners, together with money collected, was given away. To this day, in many of the little Sussex churches, there are long wooden boards on the inside walls that list the legacies for the relief of the poor which in many cases state that they are to be given on Gooding Day, December 21st, or at Christmas.

At Beeding, in West Sussex, the vicar on Gooding Day gave away the Church doles from a certain window in the vicarage. He sat there with a box of half-crowns and gave one to every old lady who presented him with an evergreen twig.

A similar custom was kept up at several other villages. Sometimes the women had to bring a twig, at other times the small branch of a tree.

The giving of these St. Thomas' doles and other money collected in church for this purpose was stopped by the Ecclesiastical Commissioners in 1853, a fact which the Rev. Mr. Warter, who was vicar of West Tarring at the time, greatly regretted. He wrote that 'the custom of going-a-gooding, or going-a-corning, on this day was of great antiquity'.

Until the early decades of this century the charities of St. Nicholas, the old parish church of Brighton, were given away on St. Thomas' day, unless it fell on a Sunday, when it took place on the Monday following. By that time they had been incorporated into what was known as The Mayors Fund, and until the time of the Second World War Brighton people received their goodies in the form of tickets, which could be exchanged with certain tradesmen for food, firing or clothing. Later it was changed to a money payment, and now, in these 'no time' days, it is sent out in the form of a cheque – all a bit impersonal.

One of the most recent Sussex bequests to be left for distribution on Gooding Day was that of Ambrose Gorham, a wealthy bookmaker, who is principally remembered because his horse *Shannon Lass* won the Derby in 1910, and another horse *Ultimus*, ridden by Steve Donaghue, won the Grand National in 1911. Gorham retired at the early age of 39 to Telescombe, a delightful little village in a fold of the Downs between Newhaven and Rottingdean. There he fashioned his life on that of an old time squire. He farmed and looked after the village and villagers in many ways.

He died in 1933 and left the whole of his Telescombe estate to the Mayor, Aldermen and Burgesses of Brighton in trust. This estate comprised almost the whole of the actual village, and a large amount of the surrounding land. There were a number of conditions, among them being the distribution of a certain sum of money to poor women on St. Thomas' day. Because of the terms of Gorham's will this is now becoming something of a problem, as the village has become almost a museum village. It is tucked away almost in complete isolation without any transport, and today there is a distinct lack of recipients for his benevolence.

Today, the benefits of the Welfare State, and inflation which has devalued the real worth of the original bequests, have rendered the old charities obsolete. But one cannot help regretting that some of the colourful customs associated with them must die out too.

The
Rites of Spring

If we were living some thousand years ago, when spring came around we would be up to our necks in ceremonies to make the year a good and fruitful one.

An important rite was, and still is, the tossing around of balls, such as community football, marbles, hurling, etc. There are numerous suggestions and theories as to the why and wherefore of these obsessions, but it is agreed by all that the custom goes back many thousands of years to the time when our early forebears changed their way of life from hunting and gathering food to the more settled life of growing crops.

Apparently the ancient Egyptians had a spring fertility rite some 4,000 years ago at the temple of Paprenis which involved the throwing of balls, and even, it is thought, human heads!

The fertility ceremony theory certainly holds good for the origin of the mass football that used to take place at Dorking, just over the Sussex-Surrey border up to 1905, though thankfully not using heads as balls! The opposing teams were not called Upper or Lower town, as is often the case where mass football now takes place, but Heaven and Hell. The people of Dorking who took part in it also wore fancy dress supposedly to represent the old gods of Britain.

There does not appear to be any memories remaining of mass football being played in Sussex, but the ancient game of bat-and-trap is still played on Good Friday on the recreation ground at Burgess Hill, and at Brighton on the Level, an open piece of land to the north of the town. Today, the game is only just alive. One match is played at Burgess Hill and two on the

Level at Brighton. Up to the 1950s there were nine or ten, and earlier in the century, the whole of the Level would be covered with people either playing or watching bat-and-trap matches. Every public house in the neighbourhood of the Level at one time possessed a trap, and all entered a team. The Bat Inn on the north west of the Level still has an inn sign showing a boy in Victorian dress, with a bat in his hand held at the ready over the trap at his feet.

Bat-and-trap is played by two sides, batsmen and fielders, with a trap, a solid piece of wood shaped like a carpenter's plane. On top of the trap swivels a spoon-shaped piece of wood. The bowl end, with the ball in it, rests in a hollowed-out part of the trap, and the handle end is left sticking up in the air. The handle end is then struck sharply with the side of the bat. This sends the ball in the air for the batsmen to hit.

Any number of players can take part. In Brighton the number is 14 a side. The pitch is marked out with a piece of rope around three sides of a rectangle, and the trap is placed on the fourth side about 40 feet in front of the fielders, who stand, or squat, along the rope facing the trap. The batsman has to hit the ball straight towards the fielders. If the ball goes to the rope on either side, he is out. He is also out if one of the fielders catches the ball and throws it back and hits the trap. If none of these things happens, the batsman scores a point and has another go. When both sides have been in, the side with the largest number of points is declared the winner.

A variant of bat-and-trap is tip-cat. This also belongs to the rites of spring and it is claimed that it is the oldest known game in the world. In the beginning it was probably more of a rite than a game.

Before the coming of the motor car made playing in the street unsafe, tip-cat was played during the spring in every town and village in Sussex. In this game instead of a ball, a 'cat' – a short piece of wood about four inches in length, whittled down to a point at each end – is used. The 'cat' was placed astride a thick piece of stick some 12 inches long, known as the 'dog' or 'doggie' so that one end was in the air. This was then struck with the side of a bat. When it became airborne, it was walloped hard so that it flew as far as possible.

There were several different ways of playing tip-cat. In Brighton at the turn of the century the most popular games were 'cat and dog' and 'cat and conjurers'.

For cat and dog, two sides were chosen – batsmen and fielders. A circle was drawn on the ground and a boy stood in the circle and hit the cat as far as he could. The fielders had to guess how many paces the cat had fallen. The one who guessed correctly threw the cat back from where it had fallen. If it landed in the circle the batsman was out. He was also out if the cat was caught before it fell.

For cat and conjurers, two circles were drawn at a certain distance apart. The game was rather like cricket. A boy stood in each circle and a fielder hit the cat, and tried to get it to land in the circle. Should he succeed the batsman was out. The boy in the circle tried to stop this and hit the cat with his hand, as far as he could. While the cat was being retrieved the two boys made runs as in cricket. If the cat was thrown back into one of the circles while it was empty, or hit one of the boys who were running the cry of 'conjurers' went up. All the players then gathered around and the cat was hidden among them. The players then split into two parties. The two boys in the circles then had to change circles without being hit.

I have been told that whenever they were playing tip-cat, one boy was posted at the top of the street to keep a look out for the approach of a policeman. When he gave a shout of 'policeman', everyone took to their heels, and in the twinkling of an eye the street was empty. Apparently long before the coming of the motor car put an end to street playing, the authorities had forbidden the playing of tip-cat, because of the many accidents caused to players and pedestrians by the flying cat. On May 12th, 1767, the Mayor of Hastings issued the following notice:– 'This is to give notice that Mr. Mayor and his brethren strictly charge and command all persons whatsoever not to play at the game called 'cat' in town as many of the inhabitants are in danger of being struck by the 'cat'.

Tip-cat is played in many parts of the world. For instance, during the Second World War our soldiers serving in India watched little Hindu boys playing it at their spring festival, and it was also seen being played in Korea, during the war there.

Some students of folklore think the 'cat' may be a phallic symbol, used in the hope that as it flew to and fro over the ground it would bring fertility to the soil.

Another spring rite is skipping. At this time little girls still bring out their skipping ropes, thereby remembering, as if by instinct, that it is time to start jumping to induce the seeds then being sown to grow sturdy and strong. From time immemorial people have jumped on the ground at this time in the belief that by so doing they could impart some of their own vitality to the soil.

The words of a Cretan hymn, quoted by J.E. Harrison, in *Ancient Art & Ritual*, shows the same idea:

> 'Let's leap up for full jars.
> And leap for fleecy flocks,
> And leap for fields of fruit
> And hives to bring increase.'

Chanting certain rhymes while skipping seems to have been an important part of the skipping rites. In Sussex the incantations, although now senseless, have survived also. Chanting is the accompaniment to skipping by all small girls. Individual skippers have innumerable little ditties which they chant loud and clear in a sing-song fashion. By far the most popular was, and still is, in Sussex:

> 'Jam, jam, strawberry jam,
> Tell me the name of my young man.
> A. B. C. etc.'

At the end of the rhyme the pace is increased to what is called 'pepper'. The letter on which the skipping broke down is the initial of the young man.

Community skipping took place on Good Friday up to the outbreak of the Second World War in many Sussex towns and villages. In the first two decades of this century it is safe to say that there was a special spot in most places which was blocked on this day by men turning heavy ropes over which young men and women jumped all in a line.

At Brighton skipping on the fishmarket 'hard' and in Brighton Place, at the entrance to the Lanes, was one of the Easter sights. This skipping took place in Brighton until Good Friday 1940. True, it was only done by that time in a half-hearted fashion by a few children. That year the fish market was put behind barbed wire entanglements to protect the town from invasion. When the barricades were removed five years later all knowledge of the skipping which had gone on for centuries had been forgotten.

If the war put an end to Brighton's skipping it revived it at Alciston, a little village beneath Firle Beacon in East Sussex. A party of Newhaven skippers, finding their usual spot barred by war defences, journeyed north over the hills to Alciston, and there in front of the Rose Cottage Inn skipped and chanted, much to the amusement of the Canadian troops stationed nearby. It can still be seen there on Good Friday.

Even if the reasons for these springtime rites have been long forgotten by the people who perform them, it is still good to know that the games themselves have survived the passage of time.

Sussex Smugglers

Since the beginning of Sussex history, its long sea coast line has been an enticement to smugglers; in fact smuggling is said to be in the blood of Sussex folk.

Smuggling is often thought of as being a party of fishermen or men of the sea, risking their lives on dark lonely shores, rolling barrels and packages around. As a matter of fact, the men who ran the greatest risk were the land smugglers, the men who had to get the landed cargo from the shore to a hidey hole until such time as it could be conveyed to London, or other large towns.

This was so risky that it is doubtful if smuggling would have been so successful without the help of local people, who if not actually engaged in it, turned a blind eye or kept their mouths shut.

Even parsons helped, some knowingly, others only when they found brandy or tobacco on the vicarage doorstep and took it in and said nothing about it. Such a one was the Rev. Webster Whistler, of Hastings, who was awakened one night to find a cask of brandy on his doorstep in payment for the use of the church tower, in which all unknown to him the smugglers had hidden their contraband.

The Vicar of Guildeford Church, out on the lonely marshes of Romney, in 1800, however, allowed smugglers to hide their goods in his church although it was a Saturday night. The men had successfully landed a cargo on the beach at Rye, four miles to the east, but word of it had got around and the customs officers had sealed off all roads. When the smugglers were warned about this they decided that there was nothing for it but to hide the contraband in the church, even if it was a Saturday.

Then arose the problem of how to keep the church shut on the Sunday. They tackled the clerk and promised him two casks of brandy for himself and two for the parson if he would persuade the parson to put off the Sunday service. The parson, fortunately, was willing and the next day a notice appeared on the church door to the effect that the parson had been taken ill, and had took to his bed, and so no services would be held there until next Sabbath day. The following day the cargo was cleared, and the parson and clerk found the brandy carefully hidden for them to find!

Farmers also were helpful. Durrant-Cooper, writing in the *Sussex Archaeological Collections* in 1858, says 'It was the custom of the farmers to favour the smugglers so far as to allow the gates in the fields to be left unlocked at night: and to broach without a scruple the half-anker of Schiedam (Gin), which was considerately left in some hayrick or outhouse.' The wives of the farmers also often put out bread and meat on the gates for the men.

Shepherds also often enjoyed a gift of brandy for their help as look out men. They would stand still and silent on the hills, apparently doing their job of watching their sheep, but when a run was being made in daylight they held their crooks in such a way that the smugglers knew whether it was safe to proceed or whether to stay hidden.

A lovely story that was often repeated whenever a few shepherds got together is about the 'silly' shepherd. It happened that one day a shepherd on the hill above Cuckmere Haven, near Seaford, saw two smugglers come up from the beach and sink two kegs of brandy into a dewpond. 'Ah!', says he to himself, 'come nightfall I'll have one of they.' Later in the day when he had folded his sheep he returned to the pond and began fishing around with his crook. Suddenly, two preventive men appeared on the scene and asked him what he was at. The shepherd, not wanting to give the smugglers away or lose his keg of brandy, answered 'Dannel it, can't you see the old moon has fallen into the pond. I be a' trying to fish her out, but I can't seem to hook her no-ways.' At this the preventive men rode off laughing heartily at the 'silly Sussex', and the not so silly shepherd got his brandy!

On all the smugglers' routes there were houses, cottages, farmhouses and inns where cargoes could be hidden in secret rooms, cellars, etc. Many of these hidey holes were so well hidden that later, after smuggling had ceased, they became forgotten, and have only come to light when the building is being demolished or modernised.

Ecclesden Manor, that lies to the east of Angmering village on the lower hills between the village and Highdown Hill, has the appearance of a gracious 16th or 17th century house, but a house has been on the site since the 15th century.

In the 1950s the Brighton & Hove Archaeological Society were invited to visit the house. The wife of the then owner, Mrs. Butcher, told the members that when the house was being renovated in 1912, a large shaft was discovered that went from the attics to the ground floor. The shaft had an outside entrance and was obviously a smugglers' secret hideout. In the old dovecot close by, a concealed hideout had been made within the thickness of the walls, and an underground vault was found in front of the barn. This had been covered with planks and then soil had been piled up on top.

A story about this house in smuggling times is that when some excisemen arrived to search the house for suspected contraband the lady of the house sat demurely sewing in the drawing room, with a bolt (40 yards) of French silk concealed beneath her crinoline.

At Pevensey, opposite the east entrance to the Castle, is a rambling 14th century house, with nineteen rooms. In Tudor times it was the home of Andrew Borde, the doctor of Henry VIII; today it is known as The Old Mint House, and is open to the public as a show-place. When the house was being renovated in 1930, a windowless room was discovered on the first floor. Its entrance had been cunningly concealed by a sliding door that fitted into the decoration of the staircase. Whether the smugglers made this room, or found what had been a priest's hole, is not certain, but Pevensey was notorious for housing smugglers, and the room had undoubtedly been used by smugglers in the 17th, 18th and 19th centuries.

Smuggling continued in Sussex in a small way into the early years of this century. Bill Wells, born in Brighton in 1907, used to play on the old fish market hard in front of The Old Ship Hotel and, as small boys will, he got to know the

fishermen and helped to pull up the boats, etc. One morning when he was in the fishermen's arch, under the promenade, the customs officer put his head in, and said 'Now then – which of you men were out last night and met a French boat?' One of the fishermen replied 'Oh! Not us. We're good people. We don't smuggle.' Whereupon the customs officer said 'I know you did. I was aboard one of your boats just now and could smell garlic.' As soon as the customs officer left, the men hurried down to the vegetable market and bought some garlic, which they brought back and rubbed on *every* boat that had been out, which properly confused the customs man! Bill also recalled that at that time the fishermen used to take out leather goods with them, and exchange them with French fishermen for wine and tobacco.

Worthing fishermen were also doing some smuggling at this time. These men used to go to Caen Bay each year to fish for scallops when they were in season. In a letter, written by George Toune, of Worthing, in the old *Sussex County Magazine*, of October 1952, he said he remembered how, in the 1920s, a good deal of smuggling went on between the Worthing men and the men of Caen Bay. He said that when the boats returned, the men were ready with plenty of boiling tar to disguise the smell of brandy if and when the customs man should arrive.

The nature of smuggled goods changes with the times. But it is very doubtful whether the drugs smugglers of today will ever have the romantic appeal to future generations as the old time smugglers have for us!

Silly Sussex
and the
Devil's Dyke

Sussex people are often scornfully addressed by folk from other counties as 'silly'. It is a title that makes Sussex people laugh at their ignorance, because it is not silly but *Saelig*, a corruption of an Anglo-Saxon word meaning 'holy, blessed or good'.

The county was given this name, according to tradition, on account of its many churches and good people. And this was the reason for the story of the Devil wanting to drown it. Evidence that this is true can be seen at the Devil's Dyke, to the north of Brighton.

It was from this spot that the Devil viewed the many churches dotted about over the wide expanse of the Weald. This, and the sound of the bells ringing, so annoyed him that he decided to come back on the next dark night – as everyone knows the devil can only work when the night is dark – and dig a ditch through the hill right the way down to the coast. Then when the tide came up, the sea would flood through the ditch and all the good people would be drowned and his troubles would be over.

True to his plan, on the next dark night the Devil began to dig and had got about half way through the hill when a good woman living at the bottom of the hill woke up. She looked out of her window and saw the Devil hard at work. Being a Sussex woman, she was noted for her intelligence, and guessed at once what was going on and so knew exactly what she had to do to put a stop to his plans.

She ran down and got a sieve and a lighted candle, then ran with them to the foot of the hill. There she lifted high the sieve, and directly behind the sieve she held the lighted candle. The candle thus threw a beam of light up the hillside which woke a cock. When the cock woke up he began to crow, when the cock began to crow the Devil looked up, and when he saw the round shining object he thought it was the sun rising and took to his heels and fled. Thus the Weald was saved from a watery grave and the people lived on to tell the tale!

The Devil's uncompleted ditch, a huge cleft in the side of the hill, can still be seen. It lies by the famous South Down Way, that stretches along the tops of the hills through almost the whole of Sussex.

Some years ago at Poynings, a village at the foot of the hill, a lady who had lived in the village all her life, as her father had done before her, said that in the village there was a story of what happened to the Devil when he flew away. As he flew up a large lump of Sussex clay got stuck to his heel (the wealden clay is notorious for its stickiness) and no matter how hard or how long he shook his foot, as he flew down the Channel, the clay stayed put. When, however, he came level with Portsmouth, he gave a tremendous kick and the clay fell off into the sea. Here it expanded and grew until it became an island that is known as the Isle of Wight. The island, though now in Hampshire, retains many characteristics that certainly belong to Sussex, such as long stretches of beautiful downland and tall white cliffs.

The Dyke Hill, scene of the Devil's frustration, came up for sale in the 1920s. An eminent Brighton man, Alderman Herbert Carden, advised the town to buy it and so preserve it for the enjoyment of future generations. The town council, however, considered that it would be a waste of money. Herbert Carden determined not to let the land go into other hands and bought it himself to save it for posterity. Later his fellow councillors realised what an asset this lovely open piece of downland would be to the town, and asked Carden to sell it to the town, which he did.

Today, thousands of townsfolk and visitors alike go every year to the Dyke Hill to enjoy the marvellous view right across the Weald. Until the Crystal Palace was burnt down, it was possible from here to see the sun shining on the glass of the palace, nearly fifty miles to the north.

A stone seat with the motto of Brighton: *In. Deo. Fidemus.* carved upon it now stands at the top of the Dyke. Underneath are these words:

His
Royal Highness
Duke of York
dedicated
The Dyke Estate
to the use of the people
for ever on the 30th May
1928

No one today can imagine what an exciting place the Devil's Dyke was on Bank Holidays in the 1910s. Brighton trams ran to within about two miles of the Devil's Dyke, and from there onwards, people of all walks of life and of all ages walked almost in a procession, everyone bent on getting to the dyke. True, trains at that time ran from Brighton station to the dyke, but money was short and most people used shank's pony.

The Dyke, when reached, was a miniature Hampstead Heath with side shows, Aunt Sallies, and hoop-la stalls. The one thing about it that most of the older generation seem to remember is the bones of the head of a huge whale that had been washed up at Brighton some years before.

But in the opening years of this century the fair was far larger and in addition there was a camera obscura, a bicycle railway, and a tent where 'Gypsy Lee', the Queen of the Gypsies, (a title it was said with some justification was true) sat and plied her trade of fortune telling. She was a buxom woman with dark curly hair, who always wore a red shawl or cloak and lots of jewellery.

A steep grade railway ran up and down the side of the hill to

the village of Poynings far below. This was quite thrilling. But even more thrilling was a ride on the cable railway. The cable car carried eight passengers, four on each side, to and fro across the deep ditch that the Devil dug! The passengers could thus look down to the green floor of the Devil's Dyke far below.

Today the Dyke is a much quieter spot. People now come in their cars or by coach, and after a short walk to view the Weald they get into their cars and drive away again. Few even see the ditch the Devil dug on that dark night so long ago because it is tucked away round the corner!

Hastings Chop-Backs

C hop-Backs is the nick-name given to the fishermen of Hastings by the fishermen of other Sussex coastal towns. It is never used, however, by local inhabitants as it is a title that the Hastings men are not proud of.

The men acquired it in the 18th century when some fishermen, known as the Ruxley Crew, who did a bit of smuggling, became rather greedy. Like many another, the more they had the more they wanted, and so they had the bright idea of adding piracy to their trade. Whenever a ship that looked worth robbing was becalmed in the offing, they would row out and hail the vessel on the pretence of doing some bartering. When the captain invited them aboard, the men would swarm up the ladder, overcome the crew, bind up the captain, and proceed to take away all the valuables and money that they could lay their hands on.

It happened one day that a large Dutch vessel lay just offshore and out rowed the Ruxley Crew. This time, however, the captain, one Peter Bootes, was prepared for trouble, and the Hastings men were driven from the ship. He also succeeded in capturing one of the piratical fishermen.

The Ruxley Crew returned to Hastings and persuaded more fishermen to come to their aid and go out with them to rescue their mate. This time the number of men was too great for the Dutchmen to master, and all of them were overpowered and tied up. The pirates then took their revenge on the captain. They murdered him in a really horrible way. He was chopped all down his back with an axe – hence the title of 'chop-back'.

Could this have been a revived version of a form of execution that had been used a thousand years earlier in Hastings? There may have been a connection in the folk memory of a particularly gruesome practice of the Dark Ages.

HASTINGS CHOP-BACKS

Although Hastings is well known as the place the Normans first occupied in 1066, earlier than this, in the 8th and 9th centuries this important Saxon coastal town fell victim to the Danish raiders. Monastic records of that time describe the Danish rite of the 'Blood Eagle' whereby the body of a victim was hacked open and his ribs splayed out in a wing-like fashion. This barbaric practice was so unfamiliar in the England of the 18th century that it surely must be a memory from those far off days.

There are many tales linking the Danish invasions with local customs. One in particular is about the game of Throwing-at-Cocks, which was played all over England until 1780, when by an act passed at Westminster it was forbidden because of its cruelty. Hastings men, however, acted in advance of this act. The town authorities in 1769, published the following order:– 'Notice is hereby given by order of Mr. Mayor that if any person or persons whatsoever shall be found throwing at cocks in or about the town or Libertys thereof, they will be prosecuted by the same as the law directs.'

The game was a cockshy, in which a live tethered cock was used, at which sticks were thrown. The man who threw the stick at the poor creature which killed it was awarded the bird as a prize. There has always been a tradition in England that the game was brought here by the Danes. It is thought to have originally been part of a festival held by the Danes at the time of seed sowing, to improve the crops.

Cock-throwing, as a matter of fact, is still practised in Denmark, though happily not with *live* cocks! It is the custom that just before Lent the sweet shops make a display of large cocks made of strong paper or thin cardboard and filled with sweets. On Shrove Monday children hold cock-throwing parties. The cocks are hung on a piece of cord stretched between two posts and children throw sticks at them until the sweets come tumbling out and then ensues a glorious scramble.

There is another tale that must have come down from those days of Danish occupation. This says that the Danes were great oppressors, and the Saxons decided that they, on Shrove Tuesday, would creep along to the tents of the Danes and kill

41

them as they slept. But on the way they disturbed a cock who began to crow and woke the Danes. The plot failed, and this game was started in revenge for the cock that crowed.

Another local Sussex practice may also go back to the time of the Viking raids and Danish settlement. This one concerns the ritual involved in the chopping down of Elder plants. Apparently the Scandinavian people thought highly of the elder tree because they believed that the great Mother Goddess was born in its branches, and that until about a century ago, Danish people always asked the elder tree's permission, three times, when they were about to chop it down or trim it. If nothing was heard after the three times of asking, the people gave three big spits and chopped at it.

In the little village of Boreham Street on the north east edge of the Pevensey marshes, a lady related quite recently how she was chopping down an elder tree in the garden when her husband came along and said laughingly 'Have you asked old Hobbeldick if you can do that? The old people around here say that if you don't do this you will have bad luck!'

With the foregoing evidence of how memories of times long past have lingered in this area, it is surely possible that it was not the evil revenge of the Ruxley Crew in 1768 that gave the name of 'Chop-backs' to the men of Hastings, but an event that took place some thousand years earlier when the Danish raiders brought some of their more distasteful customs to this part of Sussex.

Charles II's Escape to France

The 29th of May is Oak Apple Day. Fifty years ago, Sussex children still kept up the custom of slashing every child who did not 'sport their oak' (wear an oak apple or oak leaf) on the back of their legs with a bunch of stinging nettles.

In Brighton, however, the punishment for not sporting your oak was a hard pinch on the backside; in fact, the day was vulgarly known as 'Pinch-bum-day'. The reason for the nettles appears to be lost, but the pinch was done in memory of the time when Colonel Carless had to keep pinching King Charles on that spot to prevent him from falling asleep and falling out of the tree, at Boscobel, after the battle of Worcester in September 1651.

May 29th was an important anniversary. It was the birthday of Charles II, and also the day on which in 1660 he returned to London in triumph, after long years in exile in Europe during Cromwell's regime.

By Act of Parliament this day was made a universal holiday. Special prayers were inserted in the Prayer Book to be said on this day. An 1851 Prayer Book says under the order of service 'And the memory thereof .... to be for ever kept holy'.

Sussex is rich in tales about the last part of Charles' journey from the Hampshire border to Shoreham where he finally got away to France. At Racton, near Chichester, he had been given shelter in the home of Colonel Gounter, the man who made the final arrangements for the escape. Gounter rode off to Brighton as soon as Charles arrived, to meet Nicholas Tettersell, a boatman whose name had been given to Gounter as a man who might possibly help.

When Gounter got to Brighton he found that Tettersell had

started on a journey westwards but was anchored at Shoreham. So off to Shoreham went Gounter and found *The Surprise*, Tettersell's boat. After a discussion it was agreed that for £60 Tettersell would take two men who had been fighting a duel across to France. But unless they could come quickly he would have to sail as he could not risk raising suspicion by anchoring at Shoreham for longer than one day. Gounter hurried back home and early next day the King, Lord Wilmot and Gounter set off, across the Downs through some of the most beautiful country in West Sussex.

At Kingly Vale, it is said that the King drew rein and, looking down on its beauty, exclaimed that England was surely worth fighting for. At the George and Dragon Inn on Houghton Hill the three men stopped and called for a drink to wash down their lunch of a neat's tongue. This inn bears a tablet saying that Charles II called there for a pot of ale.

A tale known at Arundel is that Charles narrowly escaped capture as he and his companions came riding towards the Castle. Just as they reached it the gates were thrown open and out rode Colonel Morley, the man who was in charge of the Parliamentary troops in Sussex. The three men dismounted and drew into the side of the road to make themselves as inconspicuous as possible. They apparently succeeded for no one took any notice of them. When the King was told just who had passed so closely by, he is said to have replied merrily, 'I did not like his starched moustaches'. This rather casual reply may sound as though Charles was not worried about being captured, but it is often forgotten that Charles was only 21 years of age at the time.

Another near capture came as the three approached the bridge over the river Adur at Beeding, which was guarded by troops. A hurried conference was held as to whether to go back, but Charles decided that they should go on, and at that critical moment the rations arrived for the troops. In the commotion of these being given out, the bridge was left unguarded and the three men were able to ride over without detection.

But when a few minutes later a party of Parliamentary soldiers came riding post haste from the bridge, they were thoroughly frightened. And although the troops only jostled them roughly into the hedge and passed on, Charles and his companions decided it was better to separate. In Colonel Gounter's account of the journey, he writes 'so we parted; they where they thought safest, I to Brightemston'.

Gounter rode straight up over the Dyke Hill, but which way the other two went is only gathered from traditional tales. It is possible that the King and his companion also touched the Dyke Hill because there is a story that they were given food and shelter in a windmill on the top of the hill by a man who has been described as the God-fearing miller. (Possibly his name was Cuttress, as the mill was known as Cuttress Mill.)

This may be true and, judging from what happened later, it is certainly likely. It is a fact that later a party of Parliamentary troops under the command of a Roundhead captain rejoicing in the name of Kneel-to-God Blades, burnt the mill to the ground. Tradition says it was as a punishment because it had been discovered that the miller had given succour to the King.

At Lewes there is a folk memory of the escape from which it is thought that Charles turned aside at the mill and decided to enter Brighton, via Lewes, from the east instead of the west. Here the tale is that Charles visited Southover Grange to borrow some money from a money lender. Two centuries later, in the 1880s, Southover Grange was known as 'Mockbeggers Hall', and reputed to be haunted by the ghost of a miser. Old people have told me that when they were children they used to go to the raised pavement opposite the Grange and shout at the house and then run for their lives!

Did the money lender advance money to Charles and did he die before Charles II was restored to the throne after his years in exile – and so lose his money? If so, it could be his ghost who haunted the Grange.

This tale links nicely with a memory attached to a track that runs across the Downs from Lewes to Ovingdean, via Woodingdean, that the locals used to call Charles' Avenue. This is said to be the way Charles rode to Ovingdean where he was given rest and refreshment while Lord Wilmot rode into Brighton to see if it was safe, and to find out where the George Inn in West Street was situated.

In the 1930s the owners of Ovingdean Grange served afternoon teas and anyone taking tea was shown the 'hidey hole' in which Charles hid. A tale often told is how at the time, the mistress of the house was big with child, and she was so impressed by Charles and his Stuart charm that when the child was born it bore a striking likeness to his Royal Highness.

A vicar of Ovingdean, interviewed in the 1960s, said he had been told that a record of Charles' visit had once existed among the church records but a one-time vicar fell out with his parishioners and left the village, taking the papers with him to spite the people.

In Brighton there is an old hollow elm tree on the southern edge of the western lawn in the grounds of Brighton Pavilion, the seaside home of George IV. Fifty years ago every child who played in the Pavilion grounds knew it as 'Charles' Tree', the very one in which he and Lord Wilmot hid while Roundhead Soldiers searched below. At that time the tree was on the edge of a field belonging to a farm where the Pavilion now stands.

A lot of people now laugh at the tale and say that Charles

seems to have hidden in rather a lot of trees! But a descendant of a boatman who was on the *Surprise*, one Cornelius Shrivell, said that when she was a child her father took her down to the tree and told her it was the tree King Charles once hid in, and furthermore said his father had brought *him* down to the tree, and his father before that had done the same thing. He also told her that she must bring her children down when she grew up too. 'Therefore', she went on 'it must be true.'

Another traditional story about the escape is that when Charles and Lord Wilmot came down from the tree, they quickly slipped across the road and into The Lanes, little narrow twittens of the old town. When they got half way through Black Lion Lane, they met a fishwife with a basket of fish on each arm, which completely blocked the way. The King and his companion did not dare retrace their steps because of the soldiers they had seen, and the fishwife was not going back for anyone so, according to the tale as written in some histories of the town, the King knocked the woman down and stepped over her and on down the lane. This has always seemed to me to be an unlikely story. Anyone trying to creep secretly through the town on an October evening would not have risked knocking a fishwife down, as her cries would certainly rouse the whole town! A teacher in a school in the town has said that the version of this story in her family is that it was the fishwife who knocked the King down and walked over him. A much more likely story.

The three men, later that evening, met up at the George Inn, and at one o'clock that night they set out for Shoreham where Tettersell's boat was anchored, via Southwick. Here, according to hearsay, Charles hid in an old cottage, known today as King Charles Cottage, on the west side of the village green, while he waited for a signal from Tettersell that it was safe to come aboard. Tettersell refused to take the men aboard until the very last minute so that he could sail as soon as they stepped on the boat.

Today the wearing of the oak and the pinching and slashing is fast becoming extinct. It is a wonder that it has lasted so long. From the time of the 1688 'Glorious Revolution' when the last Stuart king, James II, lost his throne, up to the end of the reign of George IV in 1830 the wearing of an oak leaf on the 29th May was a punishable offence.

For the new Hanoverian kings of England the threat of a Jacobite rising was always in the offing, and they did all they could to suppress anything that smacked of sympathy with the Jacobites. It was not until after the defeat of the Stuart Old Pretender in 1716 and that of Bonnie Prince Charlie in 1745 that the Hanoverian kings really felt that the throne of England was secure.

Mackerel
for to
Catch

E ver since St Wilfred taught the Sussex man to fish, mackerel have brought a great harvest to the fishermen of Sussex, and its coming in the springtime was eagerly awaited all along the coast. The news that shoals had been seen off Lands End brought great joy. Some of the fishermen from the larger fishing towns, such as Rye, Hastings and Brighton, would go off down the Channel to Plymouth in early January and start to fish. They would then follow the mackerel up Channel until their home town was reached.

The Sussex Weekly Advertiser for January 1850 reported that the first mackerel boat of the season, *The Mary and Rose* of Hastings, had arrived at Plymouth and had great success. The nets were so full that they were torn, 'and it is supposed that if the dogfish had not devoured a great quantity of the mackerel in the meshes, the nets would have parted altogether.'

The real arrival of the mackerel season in Sussex was when the shoals reached our particular stretch of coast. This was generally around the end of April or the beginning of May. Many of the fishermen liked it to start on May Day itself, because then they could go to sea with their boats trimmed with ribbons and flowers.

Up to the 1930s, the excitement of the preparations for the coming of the mackerel was a part of the life of the whole community. All the fishing beaches would be alive and active. The long mackerel nets were everywhere; hanging out on the railings, laying out on the shingle, and draped over the boats. In the doorways of the arches and huts figures clad in blue jerseys stood busy making new nets, passing the shuttles to and fro with marvellous dexterity. Others would be repairing nets, and yet others going through the old nets looking for holes or damage.

Many of the shoals were caught in deep water by the large fishing boats, but what was exciting to the landsmen was to see a shoal being brought to the beach by men in a couple of boats which were generally manned by four men rowing and one man letting out the net. When a shoal was sighted about a quarter of a mile off shore, the boats would be launched and lie waiting in the shallows. The shoal would come in towards the land and then turn and go out again, then turn and swim towards the shore and so on – every time getting a little nearer to the beach. When the fishermen thought the time was right, one man would shout 'let's go' and go they did, the men straining every nerve and putting out every ounce of energy to head the fish.

As soon as the boats were out beyond the fish the net would be lowered and the boats parted company, one going to the left and the other to the right so that the fish which had been swimming towards the shore would be trapped by the nets hanging down like a gate when they turned to go out to sea again. The men then rowed back to the beach, bringing the whole shoal with them if they were lucky. If they were not lucky and the net caught on a rock and made a tear in it, the whole shoal would instantly slither through even the smallest of gaps.

Sometimes the shoal was so heavy that care had to be taken to keep the mackerel in the middle of the net where the mesh was strongest. As the boat neared the shore some of the men would jump into the sea behind it and help it on to the beach. And what a sight it was to see thousands of fish jumping furiously about, their gorgeous silver colour flashing. Mackerel really did come then in their thousands!

Within a very short time boys would appear on the scene to help haul in the net. This would earn them a mackerel or two to take home. A gift really worth having in those days when money was short. The catch was quickly packed into stout wooden boxes and taken along to the fish market, and in a short time the cry would be heard in the streets of 'Fresh caught mackerel! Fresh mackerel! Stiff necked mackerel!' And the price then was only thirteen for a shilling (5p).

All manner of customs, in those days, were kept up in connection with the catching of mackerel. At Rye, for example, the fishermen used to spit in the mouth of the first mackerel they caught. This was said to ensure another large shoal. Brighton fishermen, up to 1896, kept up a custom known as 'Bendin-in' or 'Bread-and-cheese-and-beer Days', at the start of the mackerel fishing. This was a party held on two of Brighton's fishing beaches: the fishmarket beach, and the Bedford Street beach at the east end of the town. It was given by the masters of the fishing fleet for their men, and their wives and families.

Jack (Dapper) Twaites was a boy just starting on a fishing boat when the last Bendin-in was held. In 1940, when giving an account of what he remembered, he said with a chuckle that it was always called Bread-and-cheese-and-beer Day, because that is what the meal consisted of. One of his first working days in the trade was to go and buy the Bendin-in food for his master, and to take it down to the beach. He even remembered the price he paid for it. Large loaves of bread, all hot, cost three ha'pence each, round red cheeses that weighed two pounds were sixpence ($2\frac{1}{2}$p), beer was two pence a pint (1p) and ginger beer for the children three ha'pence a bottle.

Before the party began, the mackerel nets were folded neatly and bent up concertina fashion and spread neatly on the beach behind where the party was to be held. Dapper said it was the bent nets that gave the name to the custom. But he was mistaken in this. The word came from Benediction, and the nets were folded thus for the vicar to give them his blessing.

After the party was over the boats sailed to catch the mackerel. Mackerel nets were of great length and had pieces of cork fixed to one side to keep them afloat and to show where they were set. In earlier days little barrels (kegs) such as were used for carrying spirits were used instead of cork.

When the last barrel of each boat went overboard, the men took off their hats and bowed their heads in prayer, while the master prayed:

'Watch, barrel!, Watch!
Mackerel for to catch.
White may they be like a blossom on a tree.
God sends thousands, one, two, three.
Some by their heads, some by their tails.
God sends thousands and never fails.'

The master, standing aft, then said:–

'There they goes then: God Almighty
Send us a blessing it is to be hoped.'

When the last net went overboard, the master said: 'Seize! haul!'

The prayer has come down for centuries by word of mouth, consequently, there are slight variations in the words, and on some boats the prayer was repeated line and line about by master and men. The prayer is thought to have been written by a parish priest, or by one of the monks of the Priory of St Bartholomew, which stood in the centre of old Brighton from 1180 to 1514. It certainly is a most beautiful prayer.

The mackerel fishing is now a thing of the past, and the mackerel fishers are gone. It is one of the sights that future generations will not see, for not only have the mackerel almost deserted this part of the coast but if they ever came back in larger numbers there would not be enough fishermen or their nets to catch them.

St Cuthman
and the
Stone

❧

There is a rather odd saying in the town of Steyning which states 'It always rains when Penfold's field is being mown'. This saying has its origins way back in the 8th century.

Penfold's field is thought to have been a large field in the centre of Steyning, on the opposite side of the road to St Andrew's parish church. (The site of the field is now covered by the erection of the new building of Steyning Grammar School, first founded in 1614.) It was in the roadway by the side of this field that Cuthman's invalid mother, whom he was pulling along in a little wicker cart-cum-bathchair, was thrown out when the rope over Cuthman's shoulder broke. This apparently caused much merriment among some men and women who were mowing the hay in the field. Cuthman, who was helping his mother back into the cart, called out to them 'Laugh men, weep Heaven'. Immediately a great deluge of rain fell on the field, completely ruining the crop, and ever since then rain has fallen on this day.

St Cuthman is perhaps one of the most neglected of Sussex saints, whereas in fact he should be the best known. He was the man who, from early manhood until his death, spent his life among the people of Sussex teaching them, from all accounts, to love God and their neighbours, and to follow the doctrine of peace and reconciliation. History tells us that he was much loved, probably because he was lovable. To the end of his life he was almost as poor as the people he worked amongst, but, nevertheless, he was sought out and consulted by high and low alike.

No doubt the fact that he had been a shepherd boy added to his popularity with the ordinary people of Sussex. Christopher Fry's play *The Boy with the Cart* has of late years brought Cuthman's story into the limelight. A humble shepherd lad who kept his father's sheep on the hills of the West Country, he discovered that through faith he could work a miracle, that of making his sheep obey him. Whenever he had to leave the sheep unattended, he drew a circle on the ground with his crook. Into this he herded his sheep, and telling them 'In the name of the Father, Son and Holy Ghost' that they were not to stray outside the circle, he always found them when he returned standing quietly nibbling the grass inside the circle.

One day he was sure he heard God calling him to go and teach Christianity in a place where it was not known, but it was not until his father died that he was able to do so.

Thereupon he built the cart for his mother and set out, not knowing whither he went. Little is known of his travels, though the 13th century church of St Mary in the village of Chidham, near Bognor, has a side chapel dedicated to St Cuthman, so it might have been one of the places where he and his mother rested.

The breaking of the rope and the miracle of the rain decided Cuthman that this was the spot to which he had been led, and here he would stay. In the field where the church now stands he built a hut and later a church; a church that grew and today is very lovely. It has one of the best late Norman naves in the country. Its Norman chancel is 38 feet high, and there is a 12th century font of carved Sussex marble.

But in the ninth century it was of even greater splendour and beauty. It was then truly a church for kings to worship in.

King Ethelwulf, the father of Alfred the Great worshipped here and was buried in the church, but later his body was removed to Winchester, to be placed among the other early kings of England.

Alfred the Great must also have knelt in the church. He had large estates here that stretched right down to Beeding and Bramber. Bramber was then a sizeable port, with a quay and a bridge over the river Adur that was some 170 feet long. Because it was so accessible by sea it later became a large centre of Norman administration and was known far and wide as St Cuthman's Port.

Edward the Confessor gave the church and a large part of Steyning to the monks of Fécamp, but these gifts King Harold took away. When William of Normandy conquered England he gave the gifts back to the monks.

In the field where Cuthman built his first little church there was, according to legend, a large pagan stone, around which the people of Steyning were worshipping at the time of Cuthman's arrival. It was this stone which gave Steyning its name. 'Stane' was Saxon for stone, and 'ing' meant 'people of', hence people of the stone.

Some years ago, when electricity was being brought into the church of Steyning it was necessary to lift up the bottom step leading into the churchyard. When it was raised it was found to have been marked with a rough cross. It is assumed that this is The Stone. It is more than likely that St Cuthman did the marking, to show the people that it was a Christian stone. It is possible that the stone was used to form the first altar, as was done in other early churches.

In the church porch are two pre-Norman gravestones which are thought to have once covered the graves of St Cuthman and his mother. The Stone is also here, enclosed in the church as St Cuthman would have wished; and nearby, either in or outside the church lies the saint, happy among the Sussex people that he loved so well.

Sussex Inn Games

The many games that were once played in the Sussex inns have now almost disappeared. Some are forgotten, others remembered but, alas, only a few are played today.

The reason for their disappearance is largely due to the modernisation of these inns and the demise of the public bars. These, with their hard stone floors that no game could harm, a few wooden chairs and a table or two, were large enough for any game to be played.

One game that is still played is morelles, at the Blue Anchor Inn, Portslade, near Hove. The landlady thinks it is the *only* inn in Sussex where the game is played today.

This ancient game is played in many parts of the world under the name of morris, meral, and mill or 'the mill'. It is a form of nine men's morris, and is a game for two players. Each player has nine counters which they move over a board with a maze design on it. When a player gets three counters lying side by side, it is called 'a mill'.

Nine men's morris is an ancient game. Shakespeare knew it, for in his play *A Midsummer Night's Dream* Titania says to Oberon:–

'The nine men's morris is fill'd up with mud,
And the quaint mazes in the wanton green
For lack of tread are indistinguishable.'

Shakespeare was referring to the game as it was then played by shepherds up on the hills to while away the time. A game could take as long as two hours to complete. The maze was cut by the shepherds in the turf and small pebbles were used for counters.

A game that it is safe to say was played in every Sussex inn up to the first two decades of this century was ninepins, or parlour skittles as it was often called. The games played with these had such colourful names as devil-among-the-tailors, four corners, roly-poly, and many others.

SUSSEX INN GAMES

Roly-poly was played at The George Inn, at the bottom of Steyning High Street until 1939 (this inn has now been closed). True, at that time it was a revival. In the 1920s, the pins were found by the landlord in an outhouse. They were badly battered and some were worm-eaten. He was about to put them on the fire when he discovered that some of his customers knew them as roly-poly pins, and also remembered how the game should be played. The landlord then decided to have the pins repaired, and where necessary had some new ones made, and the game became very popular.

When in play, the pins were arranged in a circle, and in the centre stood the queen, a larger pin. The object of the game was to throw the 'cheese', which looked rather like a wooden ball cut in half, with a deft spinning movement so that it went all around the circle and into the middle to knock the queen down. Some of the old hands were extremely skilful, and could make the cheese spin around the circle and knock the queen out first go.

At the outbreak of the Second World War, the landlord left the inn and because the brewers would not recompense him for the money he had spent on the pins he took them away with him. It would be interesting to know where those pins are now. They would be museum pieces today!

Another game was long-alley skittles. This has been played for centuries. In fact, it is claimed that the game was introduced into Britain by the Romans. It was played in an alley attached to the back or side of the inn, and was the father of the modern bowling alley. Without a doubt it was the advent of the motoring clientele that caused the death of this particular inn game. The land on which the skittle alleys stood in many cases has been made into the pub car park.

Incidentally, the game of nine-pins was taken to America by English settlers. By the early 19th century the playing of it by professional gamblers and tricksters was so great that New York State and Connecticut made the playing of nine-pins illegal. The owners of the alleys, however, got round this law by arranging the pins in a triangular formation and adding another pin, and renaming the game ten-pins – and so began the truly American game of ten-pin bowling.

If skittles ranked as an antique amongst inn games, its close rival was 'Ringing-the-bull'. This had not much class as a game, but as a means of getting someone to stand the price of a pint, it had its merits!

It was played thus. A player sat with his back to the wall underneath a huge bull's head with a hook on its nose. From the ceiling hung a long piece of cord with a ring on the end. The object was to get the ring up and onto the hook on the bull's nose. The ring was given a kind of jerk, so that it swung backwards and upwards onto the hook. The loser had to pay for the drinks! Local men made the game look so easy that they caught many a stranger. It was played at The Laughing Fish Inn at Isfield, a tiny village between Lewes and Uckfield when I was young.

As with many of the old games, there was more than one way of playing ringing-the-bull. The second way was a bit more of a game. It was played by several people and had some kind of rules. Played this way it was popular in mid-Sussex, around Ashdown Forest way. In this version the player stood in front of the bull, which was fixed to the wall as in the other game. Six feet away from the bull's head another hook hung from the ceiling, and from this hook hung a bull's nose ring on the end of a cord. Bull's nose rings are generally hollow but for this game they were filled with lead and weighed about one pound – a formidable object when flying about in a crowded bar. (One landlord gave this as the reason why ringing-the-bull was stopped, as it could be rather dangerous.)

To play this version, the player stood well away from the bull and swung the ring up on to the hook. To do this successfully, it was said by old hands, the ring had to be swung in a curve. Men sometimes played the game in a group, the object being to see how many times they could ring the bull without a miss. One local champion claimed that he had once ringed the bull with fifty-eight consecutive throws.

This game was played at The Green Man inn at Horstead Keynes, two miles away at The Sloop Inn, Freshfield, and at the Blackboys Inn, not far from Uckfield. Here the 'bull' was a stag's head with the hook embedded in its nose.

At the time of the Second World War, this part of Sussex

was used by the Canadians as a training ground while waiting to go overseas. The soldiers were intrigued with the game and some of them learned to play it with skill. Who knows, perhaps ringing-the-bull may even today be played in the foothills of the Rockies, the Alaska Highway, and many other places.

In the museum at Hove is a curious contraption known as a toad-in-the-hole board, which is thought to have been in use in a Sussex inn for some 300 years. This was a popular game in Elizabethan England. The board is about the size and shape of a modern dinner trolley, and it has four shelves. The top is covered with a series of hazards. Sitting in the centre is a toad with its mouth wide open, and around it is a miniature paddle wheel, two trap-doors hinged in the middle and guarded by hoops, and a number of holes screened by iron hoops.

To play the game, the men stood a little distance from the toad-in-the-hole and threw metal discs about the size of a five shilling piece, but a good deal fatter. The primary object was to get the disc into the toad's mouth. This gave a score of 100. Failing this, if the disc entered one of the other holes, it slid down a chute to rest against a number painted on the front of one of the lower shelves. The only time I ever saw this game actually played was in the late 1940s at the Bull Inn, West Clandon, just over the border of Sussex in Surrey.

Another game known as toad-in-the-hole was played at the Windmill Inn, Lewes, but it was nothing like the game at Clandon. It was played on a board about 12 inches by 14 inches, which was topped with lead and had a hole in the centre. The board when in use was propped up on a wooden stool. Here the object of the player was to get metal discs, modelled on a George III penny, into the hole from nine feet away. If the disc fell into the hole a score of two points was made and if it remained on the board one point. Toad-in-the-hole must have been the father of the modern pin table.

A game that is still played in the inns is shove ha'penny, or rather shove penny as Sussex men insist it should be called, because they play with bronze discs about the size of an old penny. At Hastings, a good many years ago, this fact caused quite a fuss when the men of a London club accepted the challenge of a Hastings club. They complained that playing with these larger discs was like playing bagatelle on a billiard table!

The game of shove ha'penny, or shove penny, is often regarded as a poor man's game. But many a Sussex Inn takes great pride in its shove penny team and its shove penny boards. There are some beautiful rare and ancient boards in Sussex which over the years have acquired a wonderful polish. Winchelsea, one of the two ancient Cinque Ports, has an inn which has a board that was made out of the sign of an inn that was taken down 200 years ago.

The playing of quoits is only just alive in Sussex. This is played outdoors with heavy flattish horse-shoe shaped pieces of iron, slightly convex on the upper side and concave on the inner, so as to give an edge capable of cutting into the ground when it falls. The iron pieces are aimed at a stick stuck in the soil, and they have to fall over it, or cut into the ground as near to it as possible. It is still played on the green in front of the Victory Inn, Staplefield, every year on Boxing Day. This annual game has become quite a feature of Christmas in this part of Sussex and many people motor out to watch the game. The players, members of the local cricket club, turn up come tempest, come snow, and finish the match.

Probably the only game of Spinning-Jenny left in Sussex is on the ceiling of the Spotted Cow Inn at Angmering. The game is a kind of roulette played on a large revolving disc fixed to the ceiling. It is claimed at the Spotted Cow that there has been an inn of that name on this site since 1540, but the game is, of course, considerably younger. This inn was once a regular meeting place for smugglers and it has been said that they used to divide up their spoils with the aid of the Spinning-Jenny game.

These games of skill and chance from a time when the local pub was the real social centre of any village have now virtually disappeared. In an age of electronic entertainment many may feel nostalgia for that age of simpler pleasures. Perhaps they are comforted that at least the game of darts today continues the long tradition of playing games in inns.

The
Great Christmas Stir-Up

There are many ancient customs associated with Christmas preparations in all parts of England, and Sussex is no exception. Here, in the old days, these preparations began on a special date.

Stir-up Sunday was the special name given to the last Sunday of the Church year, the Sunday before Advent. It is on this particular Sunday that the opening words of the Collect are 'Stir up we beseech Thee, O Lord'.

These words reminded the members of the congregation that it was time to begin the great stir-up of the mixtures for the Christmas puddings, pies and cake. The women thought about the buying and preparing of the ingredients. The tradesmen thought about dressing their windows with the exciting things of the season such as, if they were grocers, bon-bons, sugar and spice and all things nice. The greengrocers would think about whether they had ordered enough Wellington apples. These apples had very white and soft flesh and were very sour to the taste. They were the kind of apple that every Sussex woman who prided herself that she was a good cook, insisted on having for the making of her mincemeat.

The butchers would try to remember whether they had enough beef and mutton suet to put in trays in the front of their windows next day. Although most cooks preferred beef suet for the making of their puddings and mincemeat, some people whose roots were deep in Sussex considered that the suet should be from sheep, in memory of the lamb that was brought by the shepherds as a gift to the little Christ Child as he lay in his manger.

The children in the congregation were reminded of a chant

they liked to sing when they came out of church, or Sunday school, on this special day, and when they did come out they began to sing:-

> 'Stir up we beseech thee
> The pudding in the pot
> And when we get home
> We'll eat it all hot.'

In Edwardian times, many homes in the following week began the stir-up. First came the visit to the grocer to buy the Christmas fruit and spices, etc. No quick task this, in the days when every ingredient was chosen and selected with care and then weighed up by the grocer. There were no packaged goods in the shops in those days. The raisins, currants and sultanas when weighed were turned into the centre of a square of a special sort of soft blue-paper, which the grocer deftly drew up over the fruit, and then folded the paper neatly together. The ends were then tucked in, and before you could say, Hey presto! there was a neat oblong parcel. Spices and small items were turned into paper pokes, which were twisted from a small square of white paper. Every shopkeeper and assistant had to learn his particular trade, and really know what he was selling in those days.

In many homes the stir-up began by all the family sitting around the kitchen table, in the centre of which was a large china bowl, brought down from one of the bedroom wash-stands. The filling of the bowl was a lengthy task as almost every ingredient had to be prepared in some way before it could go in. Raisins had to be stoned. A sticky task, but a favourite one nevertheless, as an occasional one could be popped in the mouth when mother was not looking, and there was always the chance of sucking a sticky finger. The currants had to be washed and rubbed dry, and then rolled in flour. The candied peel had to be sliced wafer thin with a very sharp knife. In those days it was bought in the form of halves of crystallised oranges, lemons and limes. Each piece had in the centre a large lump of delicious crystallised sugar, the perquisite of any childen helping with the stir-up! Almonds had to be skinned and chopped, large lumps of suet grated, as well as nutmegs. Nutmeg grating was a hard job, when young, and many little fingers got injured.

When this job was finished and the mixture ready for the stir-up, this also had to be done according to tradition. It was stirred by each member of the family in turn. Even the smallest child had his, or her, hand guided around the bowl. Mother was the first stirrer, as head of the domestic side, father came next as head of the household, then the rest of the family in order of age.

The spoon had to be made of wood, to remind us that the baby Jesus had a wooden manger for a cradle. The mixture was stirred from left to right, otherwise sunwise, because this is the way the Wise Men followed the star. If stirred correctly health and happiness followed, but to stir the wrong way brought disaster.

The mixture for mincemeat was prepared in a similar fashion, but one or two particular traditions were followed by Sussex folk. For instance, my grandmother held that a pinch of dried and powdered rosemary should be added in remembrance of the time when Mary and Joseph were taking the Holy Child down to Egypt away from Herod's wrath. The story behind this custom is this. On the way Mary washed the babe's clothes, but there was nowhere in this lonely landscape where she could hang them to dry. As she pondered and looked around, a rosemary bush growing by the way pushed up its branches to take the tiny clothes. Ever since then the flowers of rosemary which had been white, have flowered as blue as the gown that Mary wore.

By Edwardian days most people had stopped adding raw minced beef, or mutton, to their mincemeat, but in former years the mixture was just what it said, spiced minced meat.

Frederick Sawyer, a Brighton Solicitor, who was an inveterate writer about Sussex people, wrote in the *Sussex Archaeological Collections* for 1883 that his grandmother made her mincemeat from a recipe that had been used by her Sussex ancestors for over 200 years. This consisted of 8oz. beef suet, 8oz. lean beef, 4oz. sugar, 4oz. currants, 2oz. candied peel, and six apples, flavoured with nutmeg, spice and brandy.

The baking and serving of mincepies was also carried out in a ritualistic fashion. To bake mincepies in the modern fashion in little round tins was most unorthodox. They were baked in special small oblong tins with rounded corners to represent the cradle of the baby Jesus. The filling inside, so rich, spiced and sweet, was said the stand for the gifts of the Three Wise Men.

When a plate of mincepies was being offered around, right up to my schooldays the words of invitation were 'Have a happy month'. It was held quite strongly that for every mincepie eaten that had been made by a different hand during the Christmas season, a happy month would follow.

In Victorian days, when transport was bad and many young people worked away from their town or village, there was little chance of them returning home for Christmas. It became the fashion then for twelve different members of the family to bake a batch of mincepies. One from each batch was packed in a box and sent to the absent one to make sure that they had a happy twelve months.

The Christmas cake has little tradition by comparison. It would appear to be a modern invention. In the early years of this century many Sussex people referred to it as the Christmas biscuit. I never heard my grandmother call it anything else. In this she was in fact correct. The Rev. W.D. Parish, a one-time vicar of Selmeston in East Sussex, in his *A Dictionary of Sussex Dialect* which he wrote in 1875, says 'In Sussex the words biscuit and cake interchange their usual meaning. A plum biscuit or a plum cake, means a plain cake of either of these ingredients.'

The cake with the longest Christmas tradition is the gingerbread one. The history of this is very ancient. As early as the 12th century gingerbread is mentioned. In the Durham MS dated 1299 there is mention of 'Gingebar', and if there was no plum cake stir-up, there was certainly one for gingerbread. Gingerbread men or dolls were popular at Christmas right up to the 1920s and 1930s. When the stir-up was going on, the home smelled of gingerbread, and even in the homes where there were no stir-ups, there were many baker shops to supply the need.

Many children would have expected to see a gingerbread man sticking out of the top of the Christmas stocking on

Christmas morning. One old baker (or rather he may have just seemed old to me!) who lived near my grandmother at Lewes, once said that they were not gingerbread men but Yule babies, and they were made as images of the Christ Child.

The belief in the magical properties of gingerbread is still current and many people like to eat a piece at Christmas because of the belief that it will bring good luck, or in some cases a blessing.

The people of northern Europe, from whence our early ancestors came, are great eaters of gingerbread at Christmas. In fact, in many parts of Scandinavia the custom is kept up of hanging gingerbread Yule babies, angels, and stars on the Christmas tree. I remember my grandmother saying that a little pepper and ginger should be added to the Christmas cake mixture, so perhaps this was an old Sussex memory.

The last of the traditions in the great stir-up came when the Christmas pudding was served. This concerned the putting of a sprig of holly in the top of the pudding. It is still considered essential that the sprig must have plenty of bright red berries. This goes back to the time of our Saxon ancestors of pre-Christian days. Red was the colour of the god Thor. Anything that bore his colour had his protection, therefore, the pudding was safe from evil spirits.

The month of December is still a very busy time for housewives preparing for Christmas, even in these 'labour saving' times. Perhaps it will make their tasks lighter to reflect as they work on all the customs and traditions that lie behind them.

Telling the Bees

'A swarm of bees in May is worth a load of hay;
A swarm of bees in June is worth a silver spoon;
A swarm of bees in July is not worth a butterfly.'

Old Sussex Ryme

Sussex folk anxiously watch the settling of a swarm of bees, for from this they are able to forecast their luck or otherwise. Should the swarm settle on the living bough of a tree all will be well with the health and fortune of the family. If, however, it descends on a piece of dead wood then woe betide you, for misfortune is at hand. This denotes death to one of the family.

So great was the belief in this omen in the past that people seem to have given up the ghost when such a thing occurred. A doctor at Pulborough a good many years ago used to tell the story of a woman who was expecting her first baby. Everything was fine until the woman saw a swarm of bees enter her garden and settle on a dead bough. She promptly decided that the bees had come to warn her and, said the doctor, within ten days she was dead. What amazed the doctor most of all was that neither the husband nor the nurse seemed in the least surprised. They too were sure that the bees had come to give warning.

Bees were notified of all births, marriages and deaths in a family, because people believed that unless this was done the bees would either die or fly away. This was called 'telling the bees'. The usual practise was for some member of the family to go down to the hives and knock on them three times with the back door key, and as they knocked, chant 'The master is dead', or 'The mistress is dead', or whatever was appropriate.

This custom was still carried out in Sussex within recent years. At High Hurstwood, a lady recalled that during the

Second World War she and her husband decided to keep some bees to eke out the war rations. Not knowing anything about them they sought the advice of a village man who kept bees. He sold them some bees and hives and then said he would come and settle them in. He set up the hives and then stood in front of them and said 'Now you have got a new Master and Mistress and they are good folk so sees you work hard for them'. Then turning to her and her husband he said with firm conviction 'They will be alright now'.

A gardener at Crowlink, a tiny hamlet in a dip of the Seven Sisters cliffs, near Friston National Trust car park, when asked if he had heard of 'telling the bees', replied 'Well, I 'adent afore my old dad died. He kept bees. And I was a'going down the village street (East Dean) when a man said "Have you told his bees?" No, I says, I ain't. I've got enough to do without a telling of his bees. The man replied "If you had a told them I would have bought 'em, but they won't be no good now". And they weren't – they all died.'

At Stanmer, the village where Sussex University now is, a man around that way said that a drunk stumbled into his garden and said 'I see you have got some bees. I must go and tell them my troubles.' Before he could be stopped he stumbled across the garden, put his hands on top of the hive, laid his head down upon them and began to talk. The man said he was terrified that the bees would swarm all over the drunk, but they kept absolutely quiet as though they were listening. The drunk then departed saying 'I feel better now.' These tales are so remarkable that it is hardly possible to refute the statement that there is kinship between men and bees.

The belief that the lives of men and bees are closely intertwined is a very ancient one. It probably goes back to the days of man's earliest history. Certainly one of the oldest drawings in the world, which can be seen on the wall of the Bicorp Caves at Valencia, Spain, shows a naked man climbing the face of a cliff to collect honey out of a cranny while around him are little insects that can be identified as bees. The drawing has been dated as being about 15,000 years old.

For centuries men did not know how the bees collected their honey. Some thought it was got from the air as they flew around. Others regarded it as a form of magic, and some went as far as to say that the bees flew to paradise, or the particular home of their god, and gathered it in a celestial garden. One of the early beliefs of man was that when a person died their soul entered into a bee.

Therefore, if these little insects flying around were thought to be the spirits of their dead ancestors bringing them this wonderful gift of honey, the nectar of the gods, then certainly it is feasible that this is the origin of 'telling the bees'. No wonder the bee attained such an air of importance and was treated with such regard.

The ancient Egyptians looked upon them as sacred, and in many other ancient countries images of beeswax and bowls of honey were placed as offerings before the gods; a custom which the early Church adopted. As late as the 16th century men and women in Europe offered images of beeswax on the Christian altars when they wanted to give thanks or obtain help.

Such an incident is recorded in connection with the invasion of Brighton in 1514. On a night in early spring the

French fleet under Admiral Pregent de Bidoux arrived off Brighton and the Frenchmen came ashore. Before long every house in Brighton was afire. It must have been a night of panic and terror because the townsfolk had nothing but a few bows and arrows to defend themselves with. At that date all ammunition and shot had to be stored at Lewes. At daybreak, according to the chronicler Hall, the retreat was sounded and the Frenchmen made for their foists (flat-bottomed boats) which were drawn up on the beach near where the Palace Pier is to-day.

Six Brighton men, however, decided to make a last desperate attack, and as the Frenchmen rowed towards their ships, they waded out into the sea and shot their arrows into the departing boats. One of these was a lucky shot. It hit the Admiral in his cheek. Apparently it was a bad wound, because the Admiral after his recovery, placed a beeswax image of himself with the arrow in his cheek before Our Lady at Bollyn (Boulogne) as an offering for his miraculous recovery from the wound which he had received from the men of England.

At one time Sussex folk used to wassail their bees on Twelfth Night. Jugs of hot spiced ale were taken down to the hives and amid much blowing of horns, singing and hurrahing, the ale was drunk, and in all probability the dregs left in each mug were thrown over or around the hives. Unfortunately none of the songs that were sung to the bees have come down to us today, but in the middle of the 19th century the Rev. G.A. Clarkson, then vicar of Amberley, collected the following rhyme from an old man who thought it was sung or chanted when bees were being wassailed:

Bees, oh bees of Paradise,
Does the work of Jesus Christ,
Does the work that no man can.
God made man and man made money.
God made bees and bees made honey.
God made great men to plough and to sow
And God made little boys to tend the rooks and crows.
Blow the horn!

The Shepherds of the Downs

S hepherding is, perhaps, the oldest of crafts. For thousands of years men have walked the hills behind their sheep. A silent, lonely life, but one that gave much time for thought.

Sussex shepherds are, or were, no exception. For at least 5,000 years they have walked the South Downs, behind their grazing sheep, ever watchful and alert. Most shepherds inherited a love of sheep from their fathers, and followed in their father's footsteps from time immemorial. Not only did they learn their craft in this way, they also inherited memories of a Sussex that has now disappeared altogether.

Right up to the 1920s shepherds, when leaving the fold or bringing them back, counted their sheep in a language that was all their own. No one knows from whence the numerals came. It is thought that the words could go back to a time before the Celts came to live here. If this is so, the words must have been passed on through the Celtic, Roman, Anglo-Saxon, Norman, medieval English and modern speech.

The original numerals have, of course, become sadly corrupted. The Welsh see in some of the words a kinship with old Welsh. At whoever's door the origins are laid, however, it is sure that the words have been in use for many centuries.

Here are three of the counting rhymes used by Sussex shepherds, but there are many others. The first one comes from West Sussex, the second from Southease in the Cuckmere valley, near Newhaven, and the third from Lewes, the county town:–

West Sussex – One-e-rum, two-e-rum, cock-e-rum, shu-e-rum, sith-e-rum, sath-e-rum, winebarrel, wagtail, tarrydiddle, den.

Southease – One-the-rum, two-the-rum, cau-the-rum, coo-the-rum, sin-the-rum, san-the-rum, winebarrel, jigtarrel, tarrididdle, den.

Lewes – Egdum, pigdum, cockerum, fifer, sizer, corum, withecum, taddle, teedle, den.

The sheep when being counted were made to run between two hurdles, or gates, in pairs. Thus, when 'den' was said, a score (20) would have gone through. A notch, or nick, was then made on the shepherd's nick or tolley stick. Simple!

The counts show the importance of the decimal. All agree on 'den' for ten, and the five has a similarity. According to people interested in the origins of decimals, this began when people had to count their sheep by using the fingers of each hand.

The Sussex shepherd's belief in the power of a 'shepherds' crown' to give protection in a thunderstorm, is also said to have come down from their ancient ancestors. Shepherds Crowns is the name given to fossil sea urchins (*Echinocorys scutatus*) which are millions of years old. These sea urchins abounded in the Cretaceous Period, and the chalk of Sussex is full of their fossil crowns. They are dome shaped, and have a little round spot on their tops, from which the spines of the sea urchin run down the sides. Until the cultivation of the Downs during the Second World War, fossil sea urchins could be found around the holes of burrowing animals.

Right up to the 1960s, when shepherding as it had been carried out for years gave way to the keeping of sheep in fenced pieces of the hills, or in fields, shepherds carried one of these stones in their pockets, and when the lightning flashed they held the crown tightly in their hand for protection.

A beautiful sea urchin was shown to me recently by an elderly lady. It was the one her husband, a shepherd, used to carry in his pocket when he worked the hills around Birling Gap. Many people when shown one of these fossils express surprise, remarking that they are nothing like a crown. The stones, however, are not thought to represent a kingly crown but a crown of a bishop, his mitre. This is understandable as few shepherds of the past would have ever seen a king in his crown, but most would have seen a bishop wearing his mitre,

especially before the Reformation.

Our early ancestors put these fossils in the graves of their dead. In 1933, the Brighton & Hove Archaeological Society excavated part of a ditch that once surrounded a 5,000 year old causeway camp on Whitehawk Hill, Brighton. In the process they uncovered the grave of a young woman of the Neolithic period. Close up against her were two shepherd's crowns and half of one. (The grave, arranged as it was found, is on show in Brighton Museum.)

Why these stones were put in the graves of their dead is, of course, open to much speculation. One eminent archaeologist has put forward a theory that they could have been sun symbols, and were placed in the graves to give warmth or protection to the body. From the shape of the stones and the spines running down them, they could have looked like the sun and its rays to these early peoples. For many centuries the sun god was the most important god, so if these stones were his symbol they would have been of value to the dead. It is not hard to picture someone lovingly placing these stones there to comfort and give warmth to the body as it lay in the cold ground.

My grandmother, a Sussex woman born and bred, had such a stone on her high old-fashioned mantlepiece. When asked about it, she would say with a chuckle that a shepherd's crown was supposed to keep the house from catching fire, or being struck by lightning.

The coming of Christianity brought other customs and memories that have lasted to this century. When a shepherd died, his hand was gently folded over a piece of fleecy wool. The idea behind this was that when the shepherd stood beside Heaven's gate, he would show it to Peter. Peter upon seeing it would say, 'Oh, a shepherd. Come in, I know why you have been so often absent from Church.' The last recorded case of such a burial custom was at Alfriston in 1935, but the custom quite probably continued until shepherds stopped walking the hills.

Shepherds often spent seven days a week up on the hillsides, and during lambing time they actually slept up on the hills, sleeping in little tin huts on wheels that looked like large sentry boxes. Many Sussex folk will remember such a hut standing on the edge of the National Trust car park at Friston, near Eastbourne, when lambs were being born.

Nevertheless, though the shepherds worked so hard, they had their highspots, such as sheep shearing, sheep washing and harvest. Sheep shearing in those days was not carried out by the shepherds, but by sheep-shearing gangs. These were made up of men from nearby towns who were handy with scissors or shears, such as tailors, barbers, shoemakers, etc. These men looked forward to a month in the country, meeting their fellow men and also making some money.

Each gang was made up of some twenty or thirty men, a captain and a lieutenant. The captain, who wore a gold band around his hat, made all the arrangements with the various farmers to be visited and negotiations as regards pay etc. The lieutenant, who wore a silver band, was the second in command. There was also a catcher, who brought the sheep out of the pen as required; a winder, generally a shearer who had grown old on the job, who bundled up the fleeces; and lastly the tar-boy. This was a small boy who carried a tarpot from which he put a dab of tar on the wound when a shearer had sheared too close to the skin. This kept the 'tarrifying' flies away and healed the wound in no time.

The farmers who were on the circuit of a certain gang met to agree as to rates of pay, time of work etc. A meeting of one group of such men at The Swan Inn, Falmer in 1828 decided that a breakfast of meat, bread and ale was to be served at seven o'clock; work would start at eight a.m.; mid day meal would be substantial; and supper would consist of bread and cheese and a pint of ale. There were to be two breaks between breakfast and mid day, and two more breaks between them and supper. Pay, it was decided, would be 1s 8d (13p) a score, with half a crown (12½p) extra for the captain, and a penny for the tar-boy. Normal work was expected to be forty sheep a day. No smoking and singing to be allowed in the evening.

This no singing rule was unusual, I would say, because one of the joys of the shearers and shepherds was the singing and exchanging of old tales. As soon as the sheep had been shorn everyone in the village took part in the sheep shearing feast. This was held in the largest village barn or, in some places, down the centre of the village street. Tables would be brought out from the houses and placed end to end with snowy white sheets draped over them, and as the time for the meal grew near, out of every house would emerge someone carrying a dish. In some homes the potatoes would have been cooked, in others, delicacies peculiar to the neighbourhood, and from the ovens of the baker and innkeeper would have come the great sizzling roasted meats. In Sussex, of course, a slice of suet roly-poly was also essential. When estimates for the feast were being made, it is said that this was done in yards. Different women undertook to make so many feet of suet pudding.

After the feast came the singing and dancing. One song that was always sung at the Sheepshearing Feast was the lovely *The Rosebuds in June*, which begins:

> Here the rosebuds in June and the violets are blowing,
> The small birds they warble on every green bough;
> Here's the pink and the lily and the daffy-down-dilly,
> To adorn and perfume the sweet meadows in June.
> If it weren't for the plough the fat ox would go slow,
> And the lads and the lasses to the sheepshearing go.

I heard this song on a glorious summer evening in 1934, in the perfect setting of the lawns at the back of Goodwood House. The occasion was a massed folk dance festival, and the singers were the Boxgrove Tipteers, who at that time met once a week during the winter months at the Anglesea Arms, Halnaker, just for the joy of singing folk songs. The song was sung as part of a kind of masque called 'The Sheepshearers' Feast', arranged by the Tipteers. The masque began with a procession of country folk down the centre of the lawn, led by two actual shepherds, Messrs. Ridout and Houghton, carrying their crooks, along with their two old English sheep dogs, who promptly stole the show!

Alas! No longer are shepherds with their dogs and flocks of sheep met with when walking on the Sussex hills. The last shepherd I knew, and probably the last one to walk his sheep in the old way, was the one who worked for Glyndbourne farm, up on Mount Caburn. He once said that he guessed he was likely to be the last man to do so. This was in the 1960s.

He said that shepherding was too slow and out of favour with lads today. But the real reason why shepherding in the traditional way of a man and his dog walking behind large flocks of sheep on the open Downs finally died out was due to the Second World War. With the need for producing more food to keep the nation fed, much research was carried out on fertilizing and ploughing up the tops of the hills, the soil of which had always been thought to be too poor for cultivation. Since that time great crops of oats, wheat and barley have flourished upon them, and alas, the centuries old way of life of the Sussex shepherd has totally disappeared.

The Magic Cauldron of Chanctonbury

Chanctonbury ring, a circle of trees on the top of Chanctonbury Hill, was planted around the ditch of an Iron Age Camp in 1760, by Charles Goring, who lived in Wiston House, a 16th century house at the foot of the hill.

At the time of the Roman occupation there was a Roman temple in the centre. An excavation made in the early years of this century revealed that in spite of the roots of the trees having greatly disturbed the ruins it was a sunken temple with a court. This may have been a temple to Mithras, the early Persian God whose worship became popular in the Roman Empire. The Romans built grottos sacred to Mithras. This God was very popular with Roman military and maritime men and when they introduced it into Britain it also became popular with Sussex people. From the many Roman coins found around Chanctonbury the temple must have functioned for some 300 years.

A certain John Butcher, who had spent all his working life on land belonging to the Goring family who owned Chanctonbury Hill, had many tales to tell about Roman coins found around here. His grandfather, 'Mas' Butcher of Locks Farm, under the Ring, found some when planting the outside ring of trees for Mr. Goring. John also remembered a man around 1910 finding a lot of coins when carting flints from a spot in the beeches just below the dewpond. These the man kept and sold. He used to boast that a man in the Franklin Arms gave him £14 for just one coin. This, which in those days was almost a country man's yearly wage, makes it likely that it was a golden one. Coins found and reported date from Nero (A.D. 54-68) to Gratian (A.D. 375-383). Four other coins found were minted in Britain after the Romans left.

To become a member of Mithraism, the convert had to undergo a service of mystic purification by baptism and fasting. It is likely, therefore, that priests came out of the temple in the grotto with food and drink for their followers after the initiation service. The early Christian leaders when they came to Sussex would have told their converts to keep away from the hilltop temple because it was connected with the devil. This and the memory of the food and drink given by the priests, no doubt became mixed in people's minds and resulted in a local tale. The tale about the ring is that if you go there at night and run round the Ring seven times without stopping, the devil will come out of the centre and offer you a bowl of hot soup. (In some versions it is a drink.)

The origin of the story could go even further back in time to those of our early Celtic forebears, who held large gatherings of their people at certain spots on top of the Downs. At these great meetings a huge cauldron was set up. It is supposed that this was filled with a mystic potion, and that priests of the tribe dispensed a drink of this brew to those members of the tribe who were pure, brave and true.

Not a lot is known about the British cauldrons, but on the Continent several beautifully decorated ones have been found. A large silver one had engraved pictures on its side, one of which showed a naked man, or child, being dropped head first into the cauldron. From this it has been conjectured that the cauldrons may have been used for sacrificial purposes.

Barry Cunliffe, the eminent archaeologist, said at a lecture he was giving on 'The Sussex Hills' that he thought Chanctonbury could have been one of the spots chosen for holding a meeting. He pointed out that the south-east side of the Ring would have made a perfect setting, being a natural amphitheatre.

The Southdown Way, that stretches for eighty miles all

along the tops of the hills from Beachy Head in the East to the Hampshire border, passes right by the Ring. It is known that this is a path that has been trodden by the feet of men from time immemorial. So it is likely that it was along the 'Way' that many of the early Celts came to the gathering.

At a spot about half a mile from the Ring and on the edge of the amphitheatre is a crossroads, where to this day footpaths or bridle ways, to the number of seven, come in from all points of the compass.

These paths are still walkable and many people take great delight in rambling along them. They come from the south west, at North Lancing, by the side of the Manor; south, near Broadwater Green; south west, via the Pest House, Findon; west, top of Washington Bostel; north west, via Lock's Farm, Washington; north, Buncton Cross Road; and north east, at Mouse Lane, Steyning.

To-day the landscape at the Ring is much as it was in those far off days, and anyone who sits in the natural amphitheatre and looks towards the Ring will have no difficulty in imagining a priest or priests standing by a cauldron in the centre, or a Roman priest giving a gift to someone who is thought to be worthy of receiving it.

Whether the story of the bowl of soup relates to the Celtic Cauldron, or the Roman initiation service will never be known, but the local folk tales associated with the Ring certainly live on.

Tinsley Green Marbles

A t Tinsley Green, near Gatwick, on the Sussex-Surrey border, what is claimed to be the only Marbles Championship in the world takes place outside the Greyhound Inn every year, on Good Friday.

A hundred years ago every town and village in Sussex played marbles on Good Friday; in fact, another name for the day was 'Marbles Day'. Although marbles had been played for many years in Tinsley Green, it was not until the 1930s that championships were played. The idea was the brain wave of a man named Hannam, who suggested that the game should be organised into a proper championship, and he presented the first trophy, which was known as The Greyhound Hotel Challenge Cup. In 1938 the cup disappeared and no one knows its whereabouts.

The game played here is the Big Ring. It is played on a concrete circle about six feet in diameter that is raised slightly above the ground. At the start of each game it is sprinkled with coarse sand.

The game begins with forty-nine marbles being placed in the ring. A line is then drawn in the sand, the two captains stand over the line, and each one drops his tolly from the tip of his nose. A tolly is the marble that each player uses for shooting. The man who drops his tolly nearest to the line has first go. If a player shoots and his tolly remains in the ring without knocking any marble out, his tolly stays in the ring until his next shot. But should his tolly be knocked out before his next turn then he is 'killed' and out of the game. Each game can only last for fifteen minutes or under, and the winner is the team with the most marbles in the ring.

This is but one of the many marble games that were once played in Sussex during Lent. The season opened on Ash Wednesday and finished at 12 noon on Good Friday. As soon as Ash Wednesday came around men brought out their prize

'alleys', 'bloods', and other marbles. From then on all other games were cast aside and team competed against team until the time of the final match.

The teams were usually attached to the inns, such as darts teams are nowadays. My grandfather was a marble player. His team played in the Old Navigation Pit, at the river end of South Street, Lewes, just beyond The Snowdrop Inn. It is likely that the team he played in was attached to The Snowdrop, for grandfather liked his glass of ale. He wore a little silver medal on his watch chain which he proudly told his grandchildren he won playing marbles.

In many places the Good Friday finals were played off on the porch of the parish church. In the village of Streat, all the farm people were given a holiday, really on condition that they attended the Good Friday Mid-day service. It is said that they certainly went, but they played marbles outside the church door right up to the time that the service was beginning, then nipped inside, and as soon as the service was ended they nipped out again to finish a game if it had not been ended. Some years ago, an old lady at Cuckfield said that her father, a Cuckfield man, remembered the finals being played off in the porch, and during the season the other games were played in the churchyard on the south side of the church.

The Rev. W.D. Parish, writing in 1879, said that the men and boys of his parish of Selmeston in East Sussex, played marbles outside his church right up to service time.

It would appear that this was once general practice. The poet Rogers, in *Places of Memory*, alludes to this:

> 'On yon grey stone that fronts the Chancel door
> Worn smooth by busy feet now seen no more,
> Where oft we shot the marble through the ring.'

The rule of finishing at 12 o'clock was strictly adhered to, and until fairly recently it was the rule to finish at Tinsley Green at noon. But now it has grown big and it is no longer a village affair, the championship continues until all the teams entered have played.

When the games finished at noon, many eyes were turned anxiously to the hands of the clock as they approached the closing hour. In my schooldays it was a recognised thing among boys to stop playing at 12 o'clock on Good Friday. If you could find any boys playing after this time, you were quite at liberty to jump on the marbles with a cry of 'smugs', 'grabes 'em', 'takes' or, as at Battle, 'Goblins' and claim them.

The time period of the marble season shows that the game had its origins in religion. It is probable that it was one of the pagan customs that the early church leaders could not eradicate, and so they brought it into the church to sanctify it. Early man believed that stones had a special life-giving force, and it is thought that when they planted their seeds they rolled and tossed the stones over the soil to give it fertility and so ensure them a bumper crop.

People who are authorities on this subject say that it is probable that men were rolling marbles around in Paleolithic times. Ivar Lissner, in his book *Man, God and Magic*, written in the 1960s, says that seven little white marbles were found on the floor of the Dachenhohle, a cave near Mixnitz in Styria, Austria, which were used by Paleolithic men. He also writes of 30 pebbles of a similar nature and date found in the Churfirsten mountains in Switzerland, in the Wildenmann-lisloch cave, which is now 5,300 feet up. A significant thing about these little pebbles is that they were not local, but had been brought from a considerable distance.

It is nice to know that a game of such antiquity is still played and enjoyed today. But alas! No longer can Sussex boys play marbles on their way to school, due to the amount of traffic and the long distances that many of them have to travel. In the old days the games were mainly played in the gutters and roads!

The Green Figs of Sussex

It may surprise many people to know that as recently as 50 years ago there was a green fig season in Sussex, and that figs were then grown commercially. One of the largest growers was Messrs Pullen-Burry, of Sompting, a village to the north-east of Worthing. Today, many cobbled flint garden walls line the one-time village street. These are part of a wall that was originally built to protect the fig gardens from the frequent south-westerly gales that blew across the flat open land between the village and the sea.

The soft air of this part of West Sussex and the good soil of the land that lies between the southern side of the Downs and the sea is very conducive to the growing of figs. Until 1960, another fig garden was sited in the Rectory garden of Sompting. This site, alas, now lies beneath the hard surface of a by-pass road. The fig trees in Sompting are reputed to have been planted by the Brethren of Solomon, better known as the Knights Templar, who owned the site in the 12th century.

Legend says that it was the monks who brought the lore of the fig tree with them when they came from the Continent to staff our early religious houses. The fact that the fig trees grew and prospered must have given great satisfaction to the monks. Figs to them were a necessity for doctoring the people whom they had come to serve.

The men who planted the fig trees used every part of them. The leaves were boiled with pure honey and the concoction used to dose coughs and colds; crushed leaves were applied to warts; the fruit was made into a kind of jam for use as a laxative; and dried figs were heated until they split open and applied as a poultice. Even the bark of the tree had its uses. This was burnt and the ash sifted and stirred into boiling hog's fat (lard) to make an ointment for taking the itch out of chilblains.

The monks even mixed the sap with pigments and the whites of eggs to make paints for illustrating their books. In many of those which remain, the colours are as fresh and bright as when they were first used.

The remedy of poulticing with figs has been in vogue for many centuries. There is mention of it in the Bible and it was in use until the beginning of the National Health Service. As a child I often went to bed with a hot fig pushed up against an aching tooth, and this remedy was given by Isaiah to the servants of King Hezekiah when he was sick with a boil. He said 'take a lump of figs. And they took and laid it on the boil.'

According to the 20th chapter of the 2nd Book of Kings, he recovered. A text-book of the monks, *The Regimen of the School of Salerne*, written in the 11th century, goes even further. It says: 'Scorfa, tumours, glandes, fiscus, cataplasma sedet, swine's evil, swellings and kernels, a plaster of figs will heal.'

It is certainly the case that many of the fig trees that are still flourishing were grown around the places where the early monks lived. At Tarring, now a suburb of Worthing, an ancient fig garden is still in existence. Until 1950 this was a commercial garden. Since then, however, it has become a private house, but the figs still grow in the front garden. The trees are tended by the owners who enjoy eating the Marsilles, Brunswicks and Brown Turkey figs. Lucky people!

About fifty years ago, I often went there to buy figs, especially split figs – figs that had split their sides through too much sun – as these were sold cheaper. The way up to the door of the house was through a long walled garden with fig trees growing on both sides of the path. On the left side of the path was a knarled old tree which had a label at its foot which stated that it was planted by Thomas a Becket in 1162. Some doubt has been thrown on this statement, but it could be true, as the garden must have been, in Becket's day, part of the grounds attached to the old episcopal Palace of the Archbishops of Canterbury, part of which is still standing a short distance away to the north. It is known that Becket visited Tarring.

Another tradition, however, claims that the planter was good St Richard de Wyche of Chichester, whom Henry III refused to recognise, and who roamed around his diocese for two years teaching his people how to plant and grow fruit trees, a knowledge he had acquired from his father, a Droitwich farmer. One of the people who gave him much hospitality at this time was Simon, the priest of Tarring.

In Victorian and early Edwardian days the proprietor of the Tarring fig garden served afternoon teas and when the figs were ripe it became a popular custom with residents and visitors of Worthing to take a stroll across the fields to Tarring to enjoy an afternoon tea. The price was threepence ($1\frac{1}{2}$p) for a pot of tea, bread and butter and as many figs as you could eat.

In the centre of modern Brighton a knarled old fig tree, known as the Ship Street Garden fig tree, is still flourishing. This could have been planted by the monks of St Bartholomew's Priory, which stood near here from the 12th to the 16th centuries. Another small fig garden close to the site of the gateway of this priory was standing until the 1960s when it was destroyed to make way for the building of Brighton Square.

The figs that grow at West Wittering are also in a garden that once belonged to a Summer Palace of the Bishops of Chichester. At Lewes, fig trees which could be offshoots of ones that were planted by monks at Southover are growing in the gardens of houses built on the site of the one-time Cluniac house of St Pancras Priory, built in the 11th century. This became one of the richest and most powerful religious houses ever known in England.

A fig tree on the wall of Southover Grange could also have come from St Pancras. The beautiful gardens of the Grange are now available to all, for it belongs to the town of Lewes. The house is interesting in that it was built by Thomas Cromwell, using stones from the ruins of St Pancras, when Cromwell was superintending the demolition of the Priory for Henry VIII.

THE GREEN FIGS OF SUSSEX

Some gardeners, however, think that figs were grown in England long before the Norman monks arrived. Folklorists, too, believe that figs played an important part in the spring fertility festival of our pagan forebears which they held around the time of Easter. A suggestion is that the reason why Palm Sunday was also known as Figgy Sunday is because of this pagan fig eating, which the leaders of early Church had to recognise. In order, therefore, to turn people's thoughts from the old religion they gave to the day of Palm Sunday the custom of the eating of figs.

There are several signs that figs were eaten in the spring by our early forebears. In 1972, a lady living in Sussex said that as a child she lived in Wiltshire within the shadow of Silbury Hill to the west of Marlborough. She remembered that on Palm Sunday, in the 1920s, the children of the neighbourhood climbed to the top of Silbury Hill with a bag of dried figs and a bottle of water, which they ate and drank. This, she said, was the remnant of a custom in which the adult population had once taken part.

In modern Athens, the Greeks have a saying that to eat figs at Eastertide brings the babies. The Italians say that when the fig trees are budding the maidens should be locked up! Perhaps the maidens and mothers of Sussex today may be relieved to know that these particular proverbs about figs do not apply here, especially now that the commercial fig gardens of Sussex are no more!

The Sacred Sussex Pig

The Sussex pig has been a source of joy to Sussex folk for centuries. It is said that our crest should be a pig sitting on its haunches, and underneath should be the motto, 'You may push and you may shuv but I tell'ee I won't be druv.'

The ancient Celts thought that pork was the finest of meats, a gift from the gods, in fact. To them the great forest of Andrieda, that stretched across the county from east to west for about sixty miles, was valued for the many pigs it could sustain.

The Saxons, the people who came from the neighbourhood of the Ems, Weser, Frisian coast and other places nearby, and who gave the county its name of Sussex – South Saxons – also thought highly of the pig, or boar, as they always referred to it. They endowed it with almost godlike qualities, and believed that a little bronze boar worn on their armour would protect them in times of battle.

The epic poem *Beowulf*, sings the praises of their weapon-smiths in the following way: '. . . they made it wonderously encompassed with boar figures so that afterwards no sword or battle blade could pierce it.' In Brighton Museum is one of these little bronze figures that was dropped in Happy Valley, Woodingdean, some 1,500 years ago.

Pork was the principal dish at their great Yule feast. The boar was sacred to Freya, the goddess of fertility and fruitfulness, and on the night of Yule (December 21-22) she was thought to ride across the sky in a chariot drawn by a boar with a golden hide, scattering the seeds of everything that grew, and so ensuring a fruitful year to come.

William the Conqueror also found great joy in Sussex, a county with great forests. This was not because of its timber, but for the large amount of acorns on which great black and white pigs could feed. Pig, in the shape of a boar's head, was considered by the Normans to be the most fitting dish for Christmas. This was brought into the halls of their kings on a golden dish, surrounded by a wreath of rosemary (a herb that was abhorrent to evil spirits and witches) to the accompaniment of instruments and the singing of hymns.

From then on until Tudor times a boar's head was served in this fashion at Christmas to all the Kings of England. It is said that Henry VIII and Elizabeth I both ate and enjoyed a cut from the roasted boar's head for their Christmas dinner. A boar's head dinner served with all the old pomp and ceremony to the singing of carols is still held in the Hall of Queen's College, Oxford, each year during December.

It was the pig, not the ox, that supplied the meat for the Christmas dinner in countless Sussex homes up to the beginning of the Second World War. And even today there are many Sussex people who regard pork as the proper dish for the festive feast, not the 'modern' turkey. The joint traditionally had to be a hand of pork stuffed with sage and onion, and roasted until the crackling was crisp and a succulent brown.

It was served with apple sauce, and accompanied with 'drip' pudding (a suet roly-poly cooked and cut into slices, and then laid under the roast for a few minutes to catch the last of the drips), roasted potatoes, pease pudding, baked parsnips, sprouts and a thick brown gravy. Truly it was a feast for the gods!

A century ago nearly every Sussex villager kept a pig in a sty in the back garden. The pigs were turned out each morning to wander away to find a nice spot where they could lie all day. A former inhabitant of Lewes, who was born in 1870, said that when she was at school it was a common sight to see pigs lumbering up South Street to a spot near 'the timber yard'. When she came home from school at teatime, they were just going home, knowing it was feeding time.

The keeping of pigs in those 'shortage of money' days was a kind of investment. When it was killed the pig supplied meat for a long time. Every part of it was eaten from the tips of its ears to the tips of its trotters. A cold boiled trotter was considered a satisfying snack.

In my school days the 'trotter man' came round the streets in the evening calling 'Trotters! hot trotters!' He carried the trotters in a large wooden tray on his head and stopped and called outside all the public houses on his round. I was watching him once just as a man came out from the bar. The trotter man reached up to the tray, brought a trotter down, slapped a dab of mustard on it and handed it to the customer just as it was, quite unwrapped. The customer took it and immediately began to chew along the bone with great relish, quite unconcerned about any lack of hygiene.

When a pig was killed some of the joints were distributed to neighbours. As there were no such things as freezers in those days, this giving away of the pork was a way of storing food, for when the neighbours killed their pig the gifts of pork would be returned.

A dish known as Pettitoes appeared on many hotel menus as a breakfast or an after theatre supper dish in the early years of this century. The dish consisted of the boiled meat from the trotters cut into neat finger shaped pieces, dipped in a batter flavoured with chopped parsley and fried in deep fat.

Sussex pigs in all records are referred to as big black and white pigs. From Tudor times and earlier, Brighton was famous for its big black pigs that roamed around the Steine – the village green. When Dr. Russell made the town popular with his sea-water cure, the town authorities decided to erect a small bandstand where the present day War Memorial is. A son of Dr. Russell, who considered himself something of a wit, wrote in 1765 a satirical poem which contained this passage:–

'Those pigs' replied I 'grunting loud in the corn
Round the Stand I suppose are to aid the french horn.
Those pigs and those children all trotting before us
Assist with their squeaking to fill up the chorus.'

Later Sussex became noted for another kind of pig – china ones. These were made in many parts of Sussex. Some of the best ones came from Rye as early as 1704. At one time, they were much in evidence at Sussex weddings, for drinking the health of the bride and bridegroom in a 'hogshead' of beer. The body of the pig, sitting on its haunches formed the jug and the head, which was detachable, served for a mug. The snout was flat and stood firmly on the table – 'the hogshead'. Brighton and Hastings museums have some fine specimens of these china pigs. Any found today would definitely be collector's items!

Eating
Winkles in March

In March, when winkles were in season, they were once gathered by the ton from the rocks around the Sussex coast, especially at weekends when a dish of winkles was a popular addition to the Sunday tea.

The winkle man in those days came around the street on Sunday morning calling, 'Winkles! Fresh cooked winkles!' The older generation thought that winkles were good for health, and a popular saying often quoted as the winkles were being eaten was 'Eat winkles in March, it is as good as a dose of medicine.'

In this they could have been correct. During the Second World War the Radio Doctor advised people to eat plenty of shell fish especially winkles, if they could get them, to make up some of the deficiencies in the wartime rations.

Shells have always been thought to give life, and have been a symbol of fertility. To this day in some parts of the world women still wear a cowrie to help conception. Cowrie shells are also hung up in living huts and tents so that the home shall be blessed with many children, preferably male. Aphrodite was said to be the goddess of love, and as she was born in a shell, a belief arose that she exercised her influence through anything that comes from the sea. All the old love potions that were made up by 'wise' men and women, and sold at fairs, contained shell fish of some kind.

Shells have been found on the sites of many of our old hill top fairs. T.G. Lethbridge, an authority on hill-folk, in his book, *Gogmagog*, tells of how he found part of a large cowrie shell on the site of the maypole ceremony on Orwall Hill,

Cambridge, in 1943, when it was being ploughed under war-time measures for the first time in its history. He also found three cowrie shells in the graves of women of the 7th century. Did the saying arise, therefore, from the fact that early men and women of Sussex who were not able to get hold of cowrie shells made do with winkle shells?

This is certainly a possibility. During the five summers of 1949-1953, the Brighton & Hove Archaeological Society carried out a dig high up on Itford Hill, within sight of Newhaven, to the south-west. The site, thought to have been a village, proved to have been a large farmstead of the early Celts, dating back some 2,700 years. It was enclosed by a palisade, and consisted of a number of round huts. These, from the finds on the hut floors, proved to have been used for living in, weaving, storage of grain, etc. The floor of one hut contained hardly anything other than three pounds of winkle shells. Were these shells put there ready to be distributed to the women at the spring festival? That they were not the remains of a feast of winkles is certain. If they were they would have been found in the kitchen area.

A strong belief still exists today that eating shell fish on Good Friday is lucky. The people of the Scilly Isles traditionally go winkling on Good Friday, while in Cornwall limpet pies were eaten in many villages on March 8th right up until the early 1900s. These pies were made like mincepies, with sugar, spice and dried fruit with a limpet in the centre. One lady remembers her mother saying: 'We won't go down the village today. If we do we shall be offered a limpet pie and they are too hard to chew and too big to swallow.'

One Cornish village has a tradition that the limpet pies were once taken into the church and during the service smashed on the slabs of the church floor. Surely, here is a perfect example of a pagan custom being Christianized. Fried mussels are the traditional dish for Good Friday in the Irish Free State, and Scottish folk considered all kinds of shell fish a suitable dish for Easter. The only traditional way in which winkles are eaten in Sussex, as far as I know, is plain boiled, picked out of the shells with a long pin and eaten with brown bread and butter.

Nowadays, many people regard winkles as being plebeian fare and they are only eaten by the few addicts. This fact greatly amuses the French fishermen who can get them free from the Sussex rocks in many places, and who buy them cheaply in our markets. These they sell for good prices to hoteliers and restauranteurs who serve them up with garlic and wine in cordon blue recipes, under the name of Escargot le Mer, or Escargot à la Rockes. Definitely not plebeian!

Acknowledgements

I would like to thank the many members of the Women's Institutes who over the years have approached me at the end of a talk and told me their tales of old Sussex. This book would have been far thinner without their family memories.

Many thanks also to the editor of the *West Sussex Gazette* for permission to print any material of mine that has appeared in his paper.

Finally, my special thanks go to Nicholas Battle, who has encouraged me to complete the book, and given me much valuable advice.

Lillian Candlin